Advance Praise

This is a delightful, entertaining, and informative read that I would recommend to anyone considering an extended stay in Mexico. I have lived in Mexico for over 20 years, and I found myself bursting out laughing while imagining the culture shock! Berger's frankness and humor on the ups and downs of property ownership while adapting to Mexican language, culture, and lifestyle was refreshing and insightful. This is Berger's *salsa* of memoir, so do not expect a list of what to do in every situation, but as you read, be aware of how your heart beats to the sound of the *Mariachi* and then you will know if the vibrant people, culture, and land of Mexico are calling you too.

~Sally Dominguez, Co-Founder and Director of Mazahua Valley Ministries, MEXICO

***

Skillful writing---informative, yet entertaining---just the right mix to keep you wanting more. Thoroughly enjoyable.

~Jamelle Swanson, retired teacher, USA

***

Faye Berger's *Mariachi* is a love letter to everything that is wondrous about Mexico. From her wise lessons (go for "refirement," not retirement) to the stories of Casa 4 and the cultural challenges of Mexican condo life, Faye captures the frustrations of Mexico with humor and insight, never losing sight of the richness of the Mexican culture and its people. *Mariachi* is a book that sings in perfect harmony to all of us who love Mexico. *Ole!*

~Carol Merchasin, Author of *This is Mexico: Tales of Culture and Other Complications,* MEXICO

Here is a very authentic account for anyone contemplating a move or a long-term stay in Mexico. Faye emphasizes the importance of learning the language and culture of the Mexican people...all in good humour.

~Dr. Harold Stewart, retired school principal, and Betty Stewart, retired teacher, CANADA

Mariachi!

To Wilt

Mariachi!

Running Off to Mexico...

Faye Berger

Mariachi! Running Off to Mexico Copyright © 2022 by Faye Berger

All rights reserved. No part of this book may be used or reproduced in any manner whatsoever without the written permission of the author except in the case of brief quotations embodied in critical articles and reviews.

The information in this book is distributed on an "as is" basis, without warranty. Although every precaution has been taken in the preparation of this work, neither the author nor the publisher shall have any liability to any person or entity with respect to any loss or damage caused or alleged to be caused directly or indirectly by the information contained in this book.

First Edition
978-1-952976-71-1 paperback
978-1-952976-72-8 eBook
978-1-952976-73-5 hardcover
Library of Congress Control Number: 2022909842

Cover and Interior Design by Ann Aubitz
Cover Photo: From the Collection of Faye Berger

Published by Kirk House Publishers
1250 E 115th Street
Burnsville, MN 55337
Kirkhousepublishers.com
612-781-2815

Table of Contents

	Introduction:	11
Chapter 1	The Dilemma - Lesson: Know Your Limits...Plans Change	15
Chapter 2	Mexico's Call - Lesson: Know Your Travel Comfort Level	23
Chapter 3	The Purchase - Lesson: Know the "Priceless" Factor	35
Chapter 4	"Retirement," The Word - Lesson: Know Your Fun Age	49
Chapter 5	Our Condo Family - Lesson: Know the Back Story	59
Chapter 6	*Tiempo* - Lesson: Know How Much You Like Your Watch	77
Chapter 7	Owning - Part I - Lesson: Know How Much You Like Your Stuff	85
	Trust the Trust	86
	Keeping-Up Upkeep	89
	Handyperson How-to	95
Chapter 8	Owning - Part II - Lesson: Know Your Condo Etiquette in Spanish	105
Chapter 9	Owning - Part III - Lesson: Know Your Community Doings	119
	The Setting	119
	Added Value	121

	Activities To Suit	125
	La Securidad	127
Chapter 10	X Cultures - Lesson: Know Your Inquisitive Side	131
	At the Mercy of Language and Culture	132
	On the Light Side: Mexico's Infrastructure	136
	Slower Than Snail Mail	137
	Sometimes Not So Tidy	141
	Comunicado Advances	146
	On the Dark Side: Mexico's "Bite" and More	148
	Mexico's Upper Class	155
	Others of Us (Cannucks Expats, Snowbirds)	161
Chapter 11	There and Back...by Car - Lesson: Know How Fast You Want to Get There	167
	The Haul	168
	Border Adventure	172
	On Mexican Roads	177
	In Mexican Hotels	185
	Finding the Way	189
	Another Option, or Not	191
Chapter 12	The Ties that Bind - Lesson: Know Who and What You Are Leaving, and For How Long	199
Chapter 13	The Health Plan - Lesson: Know Your Happy-Life Prescriptions	213

Chapter 14	*Viva Mexico!* - Lesson: Trust Your Intuition	223
	Epilogue	241
	Acknowledgments	245
	About the Author	247

Introduction

Nothing says Mexico like the music. Can you hear it? The brilliance of the trumpets...the sweetness of the violins...the deep-voiced *guitarro*...the strumming of the *vehuela*, dramatically calling to attention? It's mariachi! It's Mexico!

You might not yet know the sweet, enticing sounds of the mariachi, which can lull a person into a dream life at the beach. Or you might say, "Sure, I know those sounds...but what's the big fuss? Mexicans are always playing their mariachi." That's exactly my point. Hardly a celebration of any kind, a restaurant, or a small family party is without their traditional musicians—the heart and soul of Mexico. Their music, the mariachi, gives us a glimpse of the rich and colorful Mexican culture, an audio tapestry celebrating ordinary Mexican people over the centuries. If you have spent an extended time in Mexico, my guess is that the music speaks to you too.

But, music aside, Mexico isn't for everyone. Mexico is daring and risky with its dark foreign intrigue. It can be messy and noisy and dusty and hot. It almost always is complex. And let's not forget, it has a different language. Yet, Mexico for many of us travelers can be an elixir of sorts that not only soothes but exhilarates. Hold it...can this be the same place? Yes. Perhaps travel to Mexico just demands some practical guidance—especially if you are considering an extended stay. Taking the leap, finding your footing, and packing your gear requires some know-how and trust. Just as with any adventure into new territory, it's best to seek out advice. That's how I hope to assist.

Only you can decide exactly where in this world you feel fulfilled—where you dream of living the good life—the place that will fill your soul. But pay close attention; Mexico just might be the place. Consider your motives. Maybe it's just a break from routine that you need, to get lost for a bit and try a new you. Maybe it's tropical breezes you are craving. Or maybe it's just curiosity about our very different neighbor to the south, a neighbor getting a lot of attention these days for all the wrong reasons.

No matter your agenda, I suggest you try Mexico on and see if it fits. Make your own run for the border. A couple of weeks in Mexico, here, then there...you too might catch the rhythms of the mariachi. You might already have traveled Mexico and feel its rhythm. Going a step further, you might be considering a long-term rental or...if the stars are aligned, even a purchase. In that case, hold on to your *sombrero*...you need to sit up and take note. As the saying goes among long-timers referring to anything Mexican, "It's just a little different."

My personal introduction to Mexico began in the eighties by dabbling in Mexican coastal hotspots i.e., upscale tourist-driven Mazatlan and Cancun Then, for a number of years, I had a very different viewpoint: serious mission work in the interior of Mexico. From there, my focus was through yet another lens: beach property. Now here I am, decades later, needing to tell the story. And that's what this is: a *salsa* of memoir, how-to, travelogue, essay…it's just my story, mariachis and all.

When contemplating this writing project, I wavered between fact or fiction. I wondered, "How might I convey it best? How might I inform yet entertain, like a good story?" The places, the characters, the lessons—all so dynamic and integral to what I wanted to say—could be a setup for a good novel. Yet I wondered why any of my attempts to fictionalize the story seemed lackluster. Then these words jumped out at me in reading "Consider This Senora" by Harriet Doerr: "When writing of Mexico, the truth is exciting enough." And that was my answer for getting Mexico on the page: "the truth is exciting enough."

So here's my true story—you decide if Mexico is for you.

Chapter 1 – The Dilemma
Lesson: Know Your Limits...Plans Change

One particular winter, shortly after arriving in Manzanillo by car for our usual three months there, my husband and I in a great hurry loaded ourselves again into our Honda CRV to drive the exhausting 2,300 miles *back* to Minnesota. We were in emergency mode—our son was in trouble, and we needed to be with him. Meanwhile, a blizzard was zeroed-in directly on our route through the US plains. We drove late into the night in the treacherous conditions, relying on sheer will and God's grace to get us back home as quickly as possible. We made it. Our son recovered. And when he was secure again...we sought out a new, shortened trip back to Manzanillo to finish out our winter stay. That tense situation might say something about the lure of Mexico: we happily returned.

That is, in fact the same winter in Mexico we discovered belatedly that our bank accounts in Minnesota had closed—and the same winter in Mexico that a tsunami warning chased us to higher ground. What's not to like about three months far, far away in a tropical climate on the coast? These events, to be clear, were unimagined when we signed on to living our winters in Mexico. But these are the sort of crisis events that prospective long-term tourists need to consider *before* they commit on a dotted line.

We had the usual fare of warnings: violent Mexican drug cartels that are pervasive and enmeshed in the culture; banditos who may be hidden on backroads awaiting an unsuspecting tourist with a stash of valuables; bad water that, at the very least, will sour a vacation fast; and the all-too-common traffic hazards which are clearly brought to mind by the frequent crosses alongside roadways All of those warnings had not slowed us down a step. Mexico was all about the adventure.

That was the sixth winter of the eighteen we have racked up now. One night about then, I bolted up in bed with my eyes streaming tears. I blurted into the darkness, "A hell hole, that's what this is!" This was during one of my meltdowns of homesickness mixed with an unhealthy dose of condo crisis. And let's not forget menopause—jeepers, Mexico can be hot. With these multifaceted meltdowns increasing in frequency, that was the time we began in earnest discussing an alternative winter plan. But what alternative would offer the tantalizing, robust, playful, colorful-beyond-senses, soulful experience drawing us to Mexico? And all this just one border away. Please, what alternative?

Admittedly, my story is a bit of a therapeutic purge. How better to work through the emotional details and minutia of peaks and valleys than to get the story down? *The Story*, even if just tucked in a drawer for no one else to see, would be helpful in itself, like a confession of sorts, or a psychological session with self. Yet on the other hand, what if my story might actually help those of you out there with an eye on Mexico? I know you are out there.

For instance, you might decide, "Yes, a Mexican condo...that would be nice, what a good idea...let's buy it!" But wait...after reading this book, you consider further: "Buy it *only* if we get a better handle on our Spanish, and *only* if a CPA-equivalent is handling the condo books." That sort of insight. A good share of what's to follow could be helpful in that way. The rest, well, I'd like to think of it as entertaining.

My approach to this subject has been the realistic, moderate view of regular folks who might get drawn into wishful thinking about owning beach property...as in, sure, that's fun to think about, but why in the name of good sense would you do it? The risks, the hard-earned money. But a curious new perspective was thrown in my face when I discussed my idea with a classy literary agent from the East Coast at a writers' conference in Mexico. This perspective had somehow been in my blind spot. Sitting poolside at our luxury hotel, the city-sophisticated agent didn't quite have a grasp on any downside to an investment into Mexican beach property. She waited to be persuaded. "Why would a perfectly normal, practical US couple buy into this?" I suggested as a hook for the book idea. Sipping her *limonada* in that exquisite tropical setting, she could only come up with, "Why not?"

Nevertheless, this is the sort of information I had hoped to find in 2004 when my husband and I pondered our investment in Mexico. Like playing the lottery or betting on a horserace, we simply had to trust our gut feelings. How else could we do it, with Mexico being so, well, foreign? Sure, we did the obvious internet searches for buying Mexican beach property, but frankly those Google hits for the most part were accounts by various disgruntled buyers who had been led astray by fast-talking condo salesmen—stories where the property never really transferred to the buyer, sham deals, lost money, stories of that nature. Didn't want to hear that, so we looked further. Still other accounts, though not specifically dark, didn't quite match our circumstances—like buyers of new high-end condos or condos in large complexes. That's not us.

Acquaintances actually living in Mexico gave some advice via email on generalities about Mexico, such as driving protocol (a car signaling left might be signaling a left turn, or, might be telling the car behind that it's safe to pass—you decide) and instructions for purifying fresh fruits and vegetables (use a few drops of Microdyn on all fresh fruits and raw vegetables, peeled or not—you decide)—welcome information absolutely, but what about the pitfalls of, for instance, negotiating a condo repair, remedying termites, eliminating rust—or what about a tutorial on Mexican condo legalities? What about that? Plus, these acquaintances lived in the interior, not on the coast, and in single-family dwellings, not condos. Again, not us. Travel books, of course, offered only tourist sort of information on hotels and sites of interest. Where is advice for us, we wondered...the real nitty-gritty of buying a small piece of Mexican property? It's true that today, blogs can answer some of the common questions for buyers out there. Not so for us eighteen years ago.

The romance of Mexico, however—that's a different story. *Romantica.* We most definitely caught Mexico's allure in our very own travels and in the adventure stories we read by Harriet Doerr, Isabel Allende, Tony Cohan, and others. In so many aspects, we could match up our travels with the words we read and be drawn into the mesmerizing culture, caught up in magical Mexico. So we traveled and read and felt confident about being in Mexico. Comfortable to travel among the nationals. Comfortable to ask questions in our broken Spanish and, literally, find our way. Comfortable to seek out true Mexico. But, as to the sticky reality of property ownership on the coast...actually buying and maintaining a piece of Mexican real estate...as to that reality, we didn't have a clue.

The topic of Mexico always seems to conjure intrigue and risky fun. The questions we have always encountered here at home in our everyday Midwest state of Minnesota suggest an overwhelming interest for those like us who sometimes wish for a little zest in life, call it a *chile* pepper experience here or there. No matter the group, when word gets around that we have a connection to Mexico, we are sought out..."So are you the ones who have a place in Mexico?" The mere mention of anything Mexican...as in, margaritas, tropical beaches, drug lords, and most definitely the proposed "wall"...well, those topics will launch a battery of questions about just how and why we spend time there. This sort of drilling has become a given. People want to know our firsthand experience as if we're experts. We get pinned down for honest answers. Our road trip there or back absolutely shocks most and, though not actually stated, we get the feeling it raises questions about our sensibilities. Perhaps our judgment has been impaired? An altered state? Understandably, they wonder: Why would an otherwise cautious pair knowingly set out in their car, two thousand miles of which traverse a network of Mexican drug traffic? Apparently, the public generally is curious about the likes of us mavericks venturing to such a place, as if Mexico is only for those willing to risk life or limb.

Just possibly my story can ease those concerns. Mexico certainly does raise questions, now especially when that wall was pushed by the White House. Wouldn't it be nice, I'd like to think, that my story, in serving my personal interests, also might serve to inform...and to warn. Have I mentioned, we own a place?

So, whether you are looking for a winter vacation home or just looking to turn up the heat in your life for a week or two,

Mexico definitely is worth checking out. "Eternal Mexico," as photographer Robert Frerck named his collection, could be the place for you. Take note that after your first visit, the issue then might be whether you want to do this again, and again...and then extend your stay...and then consider a purchase. That question, like a begging child, will persist: Please can I have it?

But we all know that a begging child hasn't always thought things through. So before going any further into my story, let me list here why someone might be interested in buying foreign property in the first place...specifically Mexican beach property. Any one of the following considerations will do, but if you combine a couple, a few...*Viva Mexico!*...you are a strong candidate. The last several certainly can also apply to renting, especially long-term renting. And if none of these apply to you, then go ahead and vacation as you like and think no more about a purchase. But do read on just to be absolutely sure. And listen for those musical cues.

So, you are interested in purchasing beach property in Mexico. How suited are you?

Check any and all that apply to you:

___ Well-off financially...cost is no object
___ Fixed on legacy idea...Mexico for the kids
___ Looking for investment opportunity...buy at a bargain
___ Would be proud to own...life satisfaction second home
___ Prefer vacation stability...a second home in a warm climate
___ Value personal space...control of decorating and designing
___ Comfortable with language immersion...not just tourist lingo
___ Handy/crafty...good at fixing things, making do
___ Wish to bond with cross-cultural community...lifelong relationships
___ Adventuresome...like to challenge the unknown, the more the better
___ Culturally flexible...adaptable, this is how they do it here
___ Awe for coastal climate...the ocean rules
___ And, of utmost importance, as to any or all of the above conditions: Like-thinking partner in purchase...shared goals, no conflict

* **Note:** From here on out I'll refer to my husband Wilt as "Mister Will" (sounds like wheel), the endearing and formal address used over these many years by Roque, our young Mexican caretaker and good friend who can't quite pronounce Berger or the "t" in Wilt.

** **Note:** Some names are changed.

*** **Note:** We foreigners who visit Mexico refer to ourselves by various labels, similar but different: North Americans, *Americanos*, *gringos*, and those of us from *el norte*. I've interchanged these terms throughout, loosely, basically referring to us foreigners. But here are more specifics: "North Americans" seems useful when including Canada in the discussion, although the inference then is that Mexico joins South America and Central America as "Latin America." *Americanos* is often heard from the locals, meaning U.S. citizens. *"Gringo"* is a non-derogatory term, again used by the locals, referring to a person, especially an American, who is not Hispanic or Latino. According to folklore, the term was generated when the U.S. invaded Mexico wearing green uniforms, and the people shouted "Green Go Home!" We from the U.S. often misuse the term when for instance we are in a group with Canadians - as in "oh, blame it on us *gringos"* - and those Canadians quickly point out that "gringos" does not apply to them. And as for the reference to those of us from *el norte,* the distinction again can refer to both the U.S. and Canada - both from north of the border. *El norte* in fact is the reference *Mexicanos,* and for that matter, refugees from Central America, use when setting out for better opportunities in the north.

Chapter 2 - Mexico's Call
Lesson: Know Your Travel Comfort Level

One might wonder about the common sense of any foreigner buying beach property in Mexico. Aren't jokes made of this? The hazards aforementioned, tossed with yet more pitfalls to be detailed later, spell t-r-o-u-b-l-e for sungazed gringos. Yet, just that phrase "beach property in Mexico" also has a ring of the good life. And that's how we were seeing it when Casa 4 at Posada del Sol in Manzanillo, Mexico, presented itself to us in 2004. The good life.

Our one-week vacation that year was yet another trip to our favorite destination: Mexico. So close and yet so far, Mexico to us offered the perfect double-barrel package for freshening our minds in the middle of Minnesota winters: foreign intrigue and a reliably hot climate. The travel agent convinced us that the Pacific port city of Manzanillo might be worth a try, especially with the new direct flights by Sun Country. A little-known vacation spot in 2004, Manzanillo had an adventurous appeal for us; we considered ourselves well-seasoned in Mexican travels and quite capable of taking on new territory, thank you very much.

Off-the-beaten-path intrigued us. In fact, even today, some eighteen years later, Manzanillo for many remains off the beaten path and little known as a vacation spot. Whenever we explain exactly where it is that we winter in Mexico, it goes like this: "Manzanillo…," and inevitably that brings a vacant response. We continue, "It's on the Pacific, a port city, midway between Puerta Vallarta to the north and Acapulco to the south." Their expression is often still vacant, but they usually nod a polite yes. I suspect that we even take satisfaction in stumping them. Then, depending on the age of the inquirer, we add, "The movie *10* was filmed there in the late seventies. Do you remember *10*?"

And so it was, that this little-known Manzanillo intrigued us. With only a week for our winter getaway that year, we agreed, "Let's check it out." After all, it would be only a one-week investment.

Compared to the two- and three-week excursions in Mexico that had become second-nature to us over the years, this one-week getaway seemed light and insignificant really and almost not worth the hassle of travel to and from. A trip for slackers. But that particular year we needed to be slackers—we needed just an easy one week getaway to a warm place in the middle of a dark winter. We had just lost my dad, the last of our parents to go. We were low key. Had we had known, however, that this trip—this one—week getaway—would forever change our lives…well, we would have been on high alert. At the very least, I would have studied up on the psychology of life decisions and how family dynamics and losses can trigger unaccustomed behavior in otherwise rational individuals. I might have carried along a simple reminder checklist of dos and don'ts regarding life savings—as in *don't* make a hurried decision without all of the facts...all of those facts in English, please. And for crying out loud, I could have paid attention to the intuitive processes swirling in my head at any given moment. That was a year of big changes.

But I'm getting ahead of myself. Let's go back to the beginning, which explains volumes about our enamored view on all things Mexican and how we could wind up taking this sudden leap to purchase beach property 2,300 miles from home. It's one thing to put money into, say, a lake cabin, common here in Minnesota and convenient too, requiring only a few hours' drive—a sound investment by most standards. So why mess with foreign property far, far away? It's not like we have a limitless travel budget. Can the draw for a warm climate be that strong? We have friends, albeit most of the Scandinavian persuasion, who are extremely proud to stay put in frozen Minnesota those winter months and wait it out. "Why Mexico?" they ask. "Isn't it dangerous? Isn't it awfully hot?"

Our introduction to Mexico began some fifteen years earlier when we found ourselves on a short fact-finding trip with our pastor and a small group from the church. Hold on now, you wonder: A church trip started all this hype for beach front fiesta *Mexicano*, not a luxury beach hotel experience? Bear with me: The goal of this church trip was securing a Mexican contact for future "short-term missions," as they were known, for our congregation. A typical short-term mission group consists of a dozen or so people who volunteer for two weeks, give or take, to assist in whatever way a mission might need, be it constructing a facility, teaching English, or facilitating maintenance—whatever the need is. The main objective, however, is always, always to build a bond between the cultures. Our intuitive and discerning pastor was very wise to consider the two of us; he must have caught in our eyes that zest for cross-cultural interaction and a spark for high-energy adventure. "Ah hah," he likely thought. "They are sold for good on this Mexico idea."

Our previous work had been with a mission group in Haiti, where we worked on a nutrition center as we stayed in tents for the two-week project. Yes, tents. Yes, Haiti. That hands-on experience then led to plans for a second trip to that Haitian community to build an elementary school, for which Mister Will had drawn the architectural plans. But that trip would never be; an attempted coup of the Haitian government the day before our travel stopped our efforts. The airport closed. I recall sharing heartfelt hugs and tears with our church group as we *unpacked* our gear and slumped back to our homes. But perhaps it was that emotional letdown that opened us to the real possibility of a similar cultural experience a year later in more accessible Mexico. You see now the draw for trips into the unknown.

That unknown played out into another unknown, decades later, when purchasing our condo. As life experiences so often do, we find our way step by step. Only when looking back do we realize they are connected. The simple fact-finding church trip to Mexico launched us into a half-dozen years as leaders of short-term missions to the Mazahua valley, just north of Toluca, to the west of Mexico City. There, at a 300-year-old hacienda in the Mazahua valley, our group of fifteen worked to construct a playground, which would be the first ever in this large rural valley. There, we observed and learned true Mexico from the eyes of the Mazahuan people. Interspersed too with our work as the group traveled in and out of Mexico City were rich and meaningful historical lessons; our Mexican hosts, with great foresight, led us on tours of archaeological sites, military fortifications, historical landmarks, and city museums. We became absorbed in the complex and colorful tapestry of Mexico. And we learned that Mexico is a proud country.

In those mountains and high plains where we worked, we had extraordinary cultural and one-of-a-kind, life-changing experiences, the likes of which would cause any credible tour guide to say, "Wow, I want to do that too!" We were housed at the hacienda, which dates to the 1700s, literally a historical site. We had personal visits at homes in the rural communities—homes with dirt floors and no roofs. As a team we worked side by side with the Mexican craftsmen and laborers, learning even the art of mixing cement on the ground. We investigated little-known ancient ruins not found in travel books. We joined the crowds at colorful and jaw-dropping religious celebrations, one of particular note featuring displays of Disney characters alongside a giant cross of Christ, a shrine depicting the Virgin of Guadalupe, and statutes of miscellaneous saints, all set off as fireworks. Oh my, where is the fire marshal? As my grandma liked to exclaim, "Jiminy!"

Our mission group was honored at celebratory dinners of savory *barbacoa* lamb specially and meticulously prepared in earthen ovens for an entire day. We were welcomed at community festivities that featured performing children on mandolins, folk games of racing cowboys jousting with live chickens, displays of fine local crafts and traditional eats, and competing sounds of the ever jubilant, joyful mariachi bands. Fiesta!

And, we hiked. In the glorious forests of the Sierra Madres, we visited the magical winter home of the Monarch butterflies, common now and very popular in Mexico's tourism. Our hike in 1994, however, was unique: A farmer allowed our group entrance to his cattle trail, and our guide was the farmer's young son with his dog alongside. Our group hiked for two hours, high into the rugged mountains before the boy signaled a steep descent into a ravine. As if directed by an internal precursor to GPS, the boy simply watched for nature's clues. There in that ravine, that precise location within the vastness of the Sierra Madre Mountains, like a hidden magical treasure dropped from the heavens to this forest, thousands of Monarchs surrounded us. In the trees, on the ground, clinging to brush, swirling our faces as if to say hello...the effect was other-worldly. That sensation forever remains with us.

These days, due to ever-encroaching tourism, that sanctuary sadly has been transformed into a theme park, complete with lunch and souvenirs. Guided tours on horseback have demolished the pristine cattle trails, and visitors purchase face masks to protect themselves from stirred-up dust. But Mister Will and I have memories that are locked in of that pristine experience in the Sierra Madre Mountains on the cattle trails with the young boy and his dog leading us.

So you say, of course, these are nifty cultural experiences, but how do these church trips tie into condo ownership on a Mexican beach? Well, it's that process of getting there that can lay the groundwork. By the time Mister Will and I were faced with an opportunity to purchase Mexican real estate, we had developed a deep trust and admiration of the common Mexican people. We were comfortable in Mexico.

During these years, our language skills were building. Of course—*claro*—along with any foreign travel comes a new language, learn it or not. Our first Spanish words, as to be assumed, were a natural progression and necessary in these in-depth cultural opportunities with the Mazahuan people. As a linguist once suggested for learning a language on the go, use the words you need to know and expand from there. We needed words to get the job done, so that's where we started. Working alongside the locals on a construction project, the Spanish word for, say, wheelbarrow becomes handy. It's *carretilla*. Not only did we learn the words that we needed to do the job, but we learned words to interact with our friendly local coworkers. Spanish words for family, children, church, and school were tools for our relationships. Words shared between cultures are sturdy links. Often, the arduous exchanges resulted in comic relief. Context is everything. Consider the Spanish word *caliente*: it can mean hot temperature, as in hot water, but also can mean hot-blooded, as in passionate...you can imagine an embarrassing exchange. Hot weather is entirely different: *mucho calor*. And, the all-important tilde ~, the accent that transforms *año,* meaning year, to *ano* without the tilde, meaning...well, let's say it's a lower body part. Proceed to speak up at your own risk: Know the accents! The locals wanted to learn too; my Bingo game was a hit in our little English class attended by youngsters and also, to my delight, their parents.

And for a study of "Mexico the country," thanks again to those smart hosts, we were soon to understand that Mexican history is rich, complex, and really, really old, dating to 1200 BC. That's when the Olmecs, it is believed, created the first society of central Mexico, followed by the Mayans, the Zapotecs, the Toltecs, and the Aztecs. Mexico claims at least sixty-two indigenous groups! And all sixty-two groups were forever changed by the effects of the Spanish conquest. Invading ruthless Europeans made their indelible mark across the country, influencing everything from land ownership to language. This sort of background to any travel in Mexico certainly casts a bright light on seeing the various social groups. For example, the Mazauan people with whom we worked, whose ancestors had been serfs under the Spaniards for hundreds of years, were clinging to the very last remnants of their own Mazahuan language. Humbling, to say the least, as we fair people from the north came eager to teach them our English.

We saw firsthand the effects of a country with limited systems to care for the poor and sick. Women, whose husbands left their homes to find work in Mexico City and never returned, were on their own with little or no means of support raising their children and caring for elders. Those with physical impairments were left to make do in their homes in the care of their family. We, in fact, were witness to such as this when laying a floor and plastering walls in a one-room house for a young mother in the Mazahua valley. She was left to tend her meager plot of corn with her teenage son and two daughters, both of whom were blind. What were we economically comfortable Americanos to make of all this?

Our Mexican guide wisely coached our mission team: "Our people know what happened to the native tribes in the US, the injustices. You aren't here to be boss; let the people *show you* how it's done." Wise and sobering advice for working with a culture that has been oppressed for hundreds of years, don't you agree? And in that light, our group was fortunate to watch firsthand the manual pouring of a concrete roof. Laborers carried cement in five-gallon buckets up a ramp to a second level. Up and down they marched until the slab was to a proper thickness. Ironically, twenty years later, this manual technique has come into play at our very own Casa 4 on the coast. The socioeconomic lesson comes full circle.

Our small efforts to help with building projects seemed inadequate really in comparison to the know-how and skilled craftsmanship we observed in that rural community, yet we were welcomed as equals and felt at home in the humble surroundings. Our small investment into building materials initiated a huge investment into new relationships. The values of family, friends, church, and school were obvious, and that included us white people from the great north. These Mexicans were thankful for our dollars, of course, but also for the new friendships. Connections were made that continue to this day. Apparently, building bridges, not walls, is what it is all about.

Here's where I digress for a testimonial to the life-changing effects of short-term missions, or for that matter, any hands-on work with world organization efforts in another country: Sign on to one, and you can see for yourself. Forever you will be tied to that part of the world. This concept, so basic in human interaction, quite possibly could be the answer for world peace—that's the power I see. But then, this is not a new idea. Wasn't this the potential that President Kennedy envisioned in the Peace Corps so long ago?

All of our special moments during those years of short-term mission were one-on-one with the local people and all due to the thoughtful planning by our host facilitators. The indelible sights and sounds and smells, the experiences and lessons of stewardship and humility in that mountain setting, all grounded us in the Mexico we know today. This then was our introduction to Mexico.

All of this is my way of explaining how Mister Will and I came to know the Mexican people and how we carried that understanding through to many years later when we by chance were buying...in stark contrast...a condo on the beach. Comfortable in our introduction to Mexico, we forged ahead to a brand-new experience. Little did we comprehend, however, the cultural miscues that would follow. Same country, but different place, different times, different people. For instance, our Mexican condo neighbors and the Mexicans who drive to the coast for holidays are not those Mazahuan people working in the mountains of Mexico. And the everyday wage earners in our industrious port of Manzanillo, the skilled laborers, the clerks, the teachers, the professionals—they are not those Mazahuan people. This was slow for us to learn now with our idealistic expectations from the past.

In keeping with those service-oriented experiences, soon after Mister Will and I settled into our Manzanillo life that first winter, we sought out the local orphanage Casa Hogar Los Angelitos. We offered our help, in whatever way might be needed, and certainly, we assumed, the orphanage had plenty on their wish lists for volunteers such as ourselves. Aren't orphanages always short on volunteers? Not necessarily. We were assigned the last-minute task of touching up a mural for the gala fundraiser...not the basic needs-sort-of-help we had in mind like, say, tutoring in English, or constructing a shelter, or assisting in the kitchen. With an abundance of donors and team projects already in the works, the orphanage kindly turned us down for any other projects. Well, that's the difference in meeting social needs of a rural area in the mountains, as opposed to a tourist area on the ocean with many well-to-do retirees feeling the need to give. So over the years, instead of hands-on labor, our altruistic work in Manzanillo has been whittled down to attending the yearly fundraiser—ho-hum for us but greatly accepted and appreciated by the orphanage.

Not to give up on our self-directed need to help these poor Mexicans, as was our mindset, Mister Will and I pushed on with another service idea. This was a plan of our own making. Spotting a rundown outdoor theater adjacent to our running track, we took it entirely upon ourselves to re-paint it. Why not? Mister Will, the architect, had a special spot in his heart for Greek columns that needed a touch-up. We claimed this as our personal community project of giving back...and in our minds, helping the poor neighborhood. Bear in mind now, this was just us two, buying and lugging paint, climbing high ladders every morning for a week. The workers at the track could only wonder what we were up to and why. The man in charge at the track had given us the okay, "*Si, si,*" but did he really understand what we were up to? Aside from our usual Spanish greetings with them as we passed each day, considering the language barrier, we couldn't get into any in-depth conversations about the why. Many weeks later we learned that they assumed we must be part of a theater company. Why else? In the meanwhile, unbeknownst to us, the entire track facility, including the theater, was in the planning stages for a complete renovation, all funded by a powerful Korean company involved with the hugely expensive port expansion. An abundance of pesos lost in translation!

Our ethnocentric view had us, the privileged White people, dealing with the poor Mexicans. But Mexico had been evolving in plain sight. A new middle class had grown up, thanks in part to the North American Free Trade Agreement established in 1994, but also as a result of more educational opportunities in Mexico, trade with China, tourism, migrant workers in the U.S. sending dollars to their families, and even, some locals say, organized crime. US franchises began to sprout up in many of the Mexican cities. Picture this new middle class as small business owners, teachers, nurses, and other professionals with university degrees. And more later on another level: the upper class. Mister Will and I needed to become current with a new Mexico.

We do see that poor class, of course, on the fringes and especially as we travel the roads of Mexico. But in our day-to-day activities in our busy port city, we see working families much like our own. And as for those Mexicans on holiday at the coast, for example our condo neighbors, they are yet a step or two above. Yet, working with the poor was how we began our chapter of owning property in Mexico.

So it was that our short-term mission work offered a full immersion of sorts into inland Mexico, our first real glimpse of Mexican life. Forget about those luxurious vacations on the beach—we were all about serving back then. I admit I did develop an itch to expand our time away with at least a little beach time. "Like normal people," I would explain. So thanks to my insistent pleas that our yearly mission trip be rewarded with at the very least a day or two at a beach—after all, here in Minnesota we are landlocked and, after all, we were self-funding these work trips and on our own time—we extended our stays to include just that. Acapulco, Puerto Escondido, Huatulco, Puerto Angel, Oaxaca, Puerto Vallarta, Isla Mujures, and Xcalak all offered the luscious beach holiday that we crave here in the north. My sun-bathing self was pleased. And all of these side-trips added yet another chapter to our learn-on-the-go education about Mexico. Unbeknown to us, Mexico would be pulling us even deeper.

Mexico was starting to grow on us like a complicated friend. What was it about the place that always seemed to draw us back, we wondered? The slickness of the coast tempered with the richness of the interior presented an enticing mix for any seasoned traveler. That's how we saw it: Mexico as a rough-cut jewel.

So, what is your travel comfort level?

Chapter 3 - The Purchase
Lesson: Know the "Priceless" Factor

This comfortableness with Mexican travel was our state of mind in March 2004 as we waited at the Hubert Humphrey Terminal for our flight to Manzanillo—another eagerly awaited visit, but this time just a short one-week getaway from a long, sad winter. Now for the second act: As we waited in the tight quarters of the airport coffee shop, I struck up a conversation with the unusual couple at the table adjoining ours: "So, you are going to Manzanillo too?" I use the word "unusual" because the man looked to be in his seventies and his appearance was farmer-like with his elevator cap snug in place, something straight out of my small hometown in rural Minnesota. The female companion, noticeably younger, we learned was his girlfriend.

"You betcha," he said. "We are staying with my sister again - real nice place right there on the ocean, but the heck of it is, she's selling it so we have to hurry up and get our last trip." My ears twitched. I grabbed for my pen and notebook to jot down his sister's phone number and the address.

Now, to be fair, my first thought wasn't about buying property but rather looking at property. Just having the address, I planned, might be fun to locate on one of our wanderings about this new town for us, Manzanillo. We always enjoyed a challenge on foreign soil to stretch our vocabulary and our agility with the unknown. Like a game. By no stretch of the imagination, however, could this game foretell what lay ahead.

Now in hindsight, I see that a hint did surface: We stayed that week high on a peninsula with a beautiful view of the bay. Late that first night, the spirit of true Mexico that had been instilled in us in those many years with the Mazahuan people came back to us: Celebrating to the music of Mexico. Here, again, those tunes drifting up to our balcony triggered a sweetness. We got up from our bed to take a look. It was the familiar clear sounds of trumpets, guitars strumming, and a chorus of male vibratos that awoke us in the middle of that night—a full mariachi band in all its grandeur! As we peered from our balcony in the direction of the music, we saw, far below on a pier, the group of mariachis as they performed. What? Why at this hour, and why on the pier? Then, we saw in the darkness a sailboat maneuvering a turn into the harbor. We were to learn that the mariachis were welcoming the sailors at the finish of a race. As each sailboat in the regatta crossed the finish line, all 1,600-some miles from California, the mariachi band performed, no matter the time of day or night. Do you find it impossible not to smile at such a display of life?

So you see, the mariachis were in effect welcoming us too, and had I put two and two together, I would have known that something was up. I should have caught the hint: Mariachis were seemingly orchestrating our next big move.

Now then, musical clues aside, our actually finding Casa 4 didn't materialize until the end of our week's stay. We had enjoyed the week, in our usual fashion of off-road adventures, although our little game of locating the mystery condo fell short. We have come to learn through other frustrating attempts over the years that having an address in Mexico doesn't guarantee success, considering mispronounced or misspelled words and roadways known by different names. Communicating an address is part of the adventure. Consider carrying along a map and a notepad to aid in the exchange of getting the message across—that's what we tell ourselves now after failing miserably so many times. A rough drawing of the area with some words written out on paper can go a long way in communicating and bypass the clumsy mispronunciations. Of note too is that Mexicanos always will oblige with giving directions even if they don't have a clue. We have been pointed down the road many times only to find ourselves even more lost. *"Derecho, derecho,"* they point straight down the road. Our particular problem in locating the mysterious condo, we later learned, was because the boulevard address Boulevard Miguel de la Madrid is more commonly known in the community by simply *costera,* "Coast Road." Who knows, we might have solved the puzzle with a map and notepad in hand. As it was, scoring a zero in that local shorthand, Mister Will and I shrugged off the effort and readied ourselves for the trip home.

So it was that, literally, as we packed our bags for the next morning flight, our hotel phone rang. I answered: "Yes, I did leave a message...yes, we were interested in seeing your condo...but so sorry, we are leaving tomorrow on an early flight." The caller was the owner of Casa 4, and sister to my unusual acquaintance at the airport. Repeatedly, she had tried to contact us, she explained, but the message had not reached us, likely lost in translation at the hotel desk. I hem-hawed, but this woman on a mission would not take "no" for an answer. Within a half hour, she had picked us up and given us a whirlwind tour, summing up the tidy encounter with her asking price. And as if on cue, the sun set in spectacular fashion there on the horizon of the Pacific, in full view from the kitchen window of Casa 4. "Wow," we oohed.

"Really?" I turned to Mister Will that next morning as we reached an altitude of 30,000 feet and I felt free to continue the discussion. "You really want to decide so...so...fast? You really want to buy it?" I thought for sure that after a good night's sleep, this man I knew to be rational and prudent about money matters would come to his senses. Over the years I had relied on his sound judgment. Seeing a hint of mischief in his eyes, I continued my argument. "I thought we were just looking for the fun of it...you know, just looking...and anyway, I'm absolutely sure we will find a better place...someday..." You can sense that any sort of on-the-spot decision especially about a life-changing matter is just not my preferred method. I would just as soon stall until every detail is sorted out and wrapped up neatly with a guarantee clause. Remember, I worked for decades in the legal field.

But as much as I balked, Mister Will persisted and pushed. "It's about retirement!" he argued. "This could be how I manage to break from the office."

Until I heard those words "break from the office," I hadn't fully realized the weight he had been carrying. For months he had been sleeping poorly, mulling over office cash flow shortages and partner rifts. The US construction business had stalled big time, and naturally with it, architectural services. Once a joy in his heart, the running of an architectural firm now was a burden. This man I'd known never to miss a day of work—because he loved it—now could see opportunity in cutting back, a lot.

"This is exactly what we need!" he announced. And with a spark of determination in his eye, he added, "Three months—that's how long we will be gone next year!"

And we were. After some quick but thorough research back home on the pitfalls of purchasing Mexican property (and there are many), after some quick but thorough calculations on our financial wherewithal (a surprise find of forgotten savings), and after some quick but thorough analyses of our personal motivations (much-needed adventure), we were ready to make a deal.

Our savvy seller even invited us to test the waters with a weekend that next month to experience Casa 4 firsthand for the full effect. Great idea on her part. "Wow," we admitted to each other. "This really feels like us!" Almost anyway.

That's when Mister Will and I found the answer to the last nagging question: "But where is a decent place to run?" Both of us, runners for decades, automatically scoped out running space whenever we traveled. For this Mexico-style living we were envisioning, the missing piece was this running detail... I know, immaterial for most, but really if you consider the population of travelers, this is not that much different than basing a decision on the availability of golf or tennis or even a gym. Our friends recently sought out a new rental location where they have wonderful birding opportunities right out their door. For us with this running lifestyle, we knew that the sloped beach would suffice only for a short distance, so where...? I recall that I especially needed assurance that my exercise habits in this new lifestyle for three months wouldn't suffer—after all, this was to be a getaway for the sake of wellness, and wellness to me translates to daily running. The familiar term "runner's high," referring to the morphine-like effect of endorphins in our brains with exercise, is a very real thing. Just ask any biochemist or sports psychologist. Over the years, I have come to rely on my endorphin fix, so when the seller informed us about an outdoor track just a few blocks away, well, the deal in my mind was pretty much clinched. Mister Will heartily agreed.

During this same weekend of testing Casa 4, we were introduced to our very first Mexicano acquaintance in Manzanillo and a key player in our Posada experience: Roque, that caretaker and friend I mentioned. Young, energetic, hardworking, and talented, Roque is our all-around handyman with an easy smile. He absolutely loves Posada del Sol, you can just tell, especially by the care he takes with the details of maintenance and beautiful landscaping just as any proud homeowner. His artistic talent is even on display with whimsical topiary designs, so adored in Mexico. How could he know those many years ago when we became acquainted that Mister Will and I picked up on that love for the place which we saw in his manner—we were trusting him, along with the Good Lord, for our big decision. If Roque was the caretaker, we were in. Our closing papers were signed within three months of our fateful first trip to Manzanillo.

But wait, wait! That decision was entirely too fast, especially for the two of us, leaning to well-thought-out money matters, as we were raised. Mister Will, born at the end of the Depression, and I, a baby boomer, were taught to work hard and save money, not spend it on foolish things and certainly not on risky unknowns, especially in a foreign country. How could we be this audacious? This impulsive? This extravagant? This so un-Minnesotan? The incongruity of our impromptu decision even now is a wonder.

In hindsight, of course as happens to us all, one can easily see the build-up for such erratic behavior on our part. All those work years, day in and day out, we slogged on, rewarded each year by a bit of Mexican travel in the dead of a Minnesota winter. Each winter as we stepped from the plane, the pure luxury of smelling the earth again was intoxicating and addicting. And, with diversity of cultures our comfort zone, we were oblivious to any danger or discomfort or distrust in a foreign land. Rather, we wished for challenges. Our dream was to be those people who make a leap. The laid-back couples we quietly observed, obviously so at home in their Mexican surroundings as to converse with ease to the waiters—"*Si, con queso, pero sin tocino, por favor, senor*"—relaxed, carefree in their sandals and airy cotton clothes, with easy-going hair and sun-drenched skin: that's who we wanted to be.

Laid-back wasn't in the equation for us in the nineties when our first Mexico trips began, with teens still at home and aging parents relying on our close contact. Our mission trips were sandwiched in, yes, but not without stress. Wandering off to remote, rural Mexico where telephone lines were few and far between, if not cut, our contact with the real world was mightily compromised. Remember, this was well before email and cell phones. Tell me: Is this responsible behavior for parents of teenagers and is this responsible behavior for adult children in care of aging parents? Even the cover of church work doesn't negate our less-than-responsible choices at that time in our lives. Somehow, with the help of loving, overseeing friends and family, and by the grace of God, our children and parents got by. But worrisome travel comes to mind. And guilt. Even after the kids were well on their own, our parents' care, ever increasing, took up the slack, and then some. Frequent car trips to our respective hometowns to assist Mom or Dad in whatever way, that became our calling. That was where we needed to be, then.

But our Manzanillo trip in 2004 signaled a new page in our lives. Our dear, lovely parents sadly were gone, our children were launched, our jobs had turned tiresome, our search for adventure had necessarily been whittled down. Enter Posada del Sol Casa 4.

Ah, Posada del Sol Casa 4....not exactly top-of-the-line, tired even, dating to the sixties, but definitely with possibilities. Really, really old Casa 4 presented as a sound, one-story structure, and certainly functional. But, as we first saw it, crammed as it was with old furniture and decorative pieces and surrounded by busy murals, the place needed an update by several decades, no question. We didn't bat an eye. Instead, our eyes locked in a transfixed sizzle as the seller went on about this and that detail and as we each imagined and mentally took notes of how this Casa 4 might be transformed into our Casa 4. Ah, hah...we thought. Potential.

So then to be clear, Mister Will and I were not buying into a top-end beach condo... not our style or pocketbook, no way. Posada del Sol Casa 4 is a far cry even from modern. That word "potential" was going to be our code for "Hey, aren't we smart to find a real deal with just a little fix-up!" Our improvements over the years have been modest in keeping with our basic draw to this property: simple, no fuss, inexpensive but, ah, in good taste. Just a coat of paint, accents here and there, upholstery updates—even these basic changes gave us a pride in ownership, yet didn't tie us down to any long-term, expensive remodel. Not prudent, we thought, to overdo, going back to our conservative upbringings. We had what I have come to know as "midwestern good-enough practicality." Excessive spending seemed over the top for this, our beach home in Mexico, when our home in Minnesota could have used several updates itself. Foremost, we wanted to be available for any guests who might venture down. "Here we are, ready for guests!" was our thinking.

Basic as Casa 4 has been over the years, only just recently I had occasion to see it in a new lens. Our realtor used the

Spanish word "*coqueto*" in describing our modest accommodation. I needed to check my Spanish dictionary: *Coqueto* means "flirtatious," which of course tickled me and casts our Casa 4 in a brand-new light.

Nevertheless, flirtatious or not, over the years when preparing visitors for their stay, I have offered the following description, lest they expect too much: "Think sixties motel with ten units around a pool." Mister Will objects strongly when I say it like that...after all, this being our Mexican investment, he's proud...but I worry that our visitors will be disappointed. Set the bar low, I say.

To be fair and not so Minnesota-modest, there is the slight detail that the Pacific Ocean is just a few steps away from Casa 4. That fact alone, one could argue, makes it very, very attractive. At least, anyone from a northern climate far, far away from any ocean will say so. The astounding Pacific in all its immensity, its power, its soothing rhythms, its shimmering beauty, will mesmerize in a sound bite. So, not to dismiss a very basic selling feature, there *is* the ocean detail.

Our ocean detail is a bit different than the next bay up...and this made all the difference in our draw to the property. The two bays stretch north from the harbor at downtown Manzanillo. The first bay is a bit rough with a sloping beach, deep sand, big waves, and very few beach vendors. This is the bay where container ships are waiting to load or unload. This is our bay. The second bay, in stark contrast, known for its flat beach and gold-flecked sand, is the go-to umbrella beach for boogie-boarding, gentle walks, and bartering with beach vendors. This second bay is always a destination when we have guests. Noteworthy too, the flat, gold-speckled beach also draws a majority of high-end condo buyers.

The fact that our Posada del Sol sits smack in the center of a three-mile-long bay with very few people on the beach on any given day makes our location perfect for us. We do share this setting with restaurants, other condos, and even some retailers that line the bay, but basically, we see the beach as ours. I can pitch my little umbrella in the sand, sit myself down on my beach chair, and stare at the waves without interruption for as long as I can take the heat. Looking first one direction down the bay, then the other, I will see only a smattering of people. Our beach.

So then, the condo...this non-luxurious, no-frills condo with its seductive power: Casa 4 is old, vintage even, in a touristy Mexican sort of way. The "Mexican sort of way" just pinpoints certain unrefined characteristics of old Mexico, as in rough surfaces, small rooms, substandard light fixtures, substandard plumbing fixtures. These sort of characteristics can actually win over those who dearly love Mexico, much like here in the north woods finding comfort in an old sparse cabin. And truthfully, Posada del Sol, dating back five decades, was built as a motel. So, you say, where's the real attraction?

The attraction might be the absence of refinement. Quite possibly, the really dated Casa 4 we saw had two main factors going for it: It fit nicely into our budget...much to our surprise...and it fit nicely into our conservative psyche. Forget about frills...this would be our Mexican escape. The idea of going against the grain of high-priced and trendy seemed to fuel our purchase. "This, friends, is who we are!"

And now for the realtor-type rundown: Space-wise, Casa 4 functions nicely with its two bedrooms, 1-1/2 baths, small seating area, full kitchen, and large patio, all squeezed into 800 square feet on ground level. The jalousie windows, at the time of purchase, though time-worn, offered a tropical touch with their louvered panes, and one might even consider this detail as romantic if conjuring up images from, say, a Bogart film and if not concerned with a tight seal. More later about the importance of a tight seal.

Function-wise, Casa 4 scores above average, and it's the large patio that ratchets up the score. Even a hint of luxury can be made because of the patio. Larger than the usual upper-level balconies in the newer condominiums, the old-style Casa 4 patio provides space for a seating area in addition to the normal patio table area. And the patio is only six steps away from a better-than-average pool and a better-than-average green space fitting for our hammock. The common areas are graced with palm trees, bougainvillea, hibiscus, desert rose, and the lovely little *terisita,* so hardy to bloom almost anywhere. Vacation pleasure at every turn, literally, that's the idea.

Yes, amen to the large patio. As we considered the pros and cons of this unfolding opportunity, sure, Mister Will and I might have had hesitation about the rough edges of this Casa 4, as in the worn windows and tired appliances, but most definitely and without a doubt, we pictured ourselves on this very patio, and very soon, with feet up, whiling away our time in the temperate air of ocean breezes and filtered sun and soothing sounds of waves. Here's that romance factor working big time. Outside is what it's all about in Mexico, we agreed. The interior space can evolve, well, *mañana,* was our thinking. This patio would be our luxury space, our indulgence in a Pacific setting. Please, *el presidente* of retirement living, just give us this little piece of real estate, this 800-square foot plot of Mexican beach property, and we're home! The image is so powerful that, as I write, I'm swaying as if with the *palmas.*

Back in the real world, the buckling down to the business deal wasn't as easy as dreaming of life on our patio. This fast and furious showing of Casa 4 on that week's getaway was all we had to go on. It's what we based our decision upon to come back for another look. It's what Mister Will photographed and I scribbled in my notes—the dimensions, the layout, the details of a twenty-minute rundown of this beach property in little-known Manzanillo, Mexico, on the Pacific coast, some 2,300 miles from home. The alarming fact is that this quick run-through would, in fact be the shaky foundation for our retirement investment in Mexico, thus far unimagined. Yes, an alarm should have sounded! A life decision of this sort in any other circumstance could easily tally up years of research. To be sure, a retirement investment is no small consideration, no matter who and no matter where, and when the investment involves foreign property, well, the common advice seems to be "Watch out!" Hard-earned money tucked away for decades suddenly is on the line. And by all accounts of retirement considerations, the subject itself can be an endless loop....where, when, how much, where, when, how much... So to look at the positive, get-things-done side, ours at least was a quick decision. "Fate!" we explain as we throw up our arms as if to announce to anyone questioning our sanity. "What else could we do? The opportunity was in our face!" But back to good common sense...what exactly did we get ourselves into?

As if this scenario isn't enough to wonder about our simplistic and naive approach to purchasing foreign property, add this: We did not even know enough to ask basic questions about the soundness of the condo organization. A crucial piece that was *not* included in the twenty-minute rundown was the odd, even bizarre, history of Posada del Sol, yet to be unearthed. The mismanagement, the looming debts, the state of disrepair, oh the stories. But for us, so naive and awestruck with the notion of owning Mexican beach property...any Mexican beach property...the foresight of questioning Posada's history wasn't on our radar. The history, however, would have given us pause. The history would have revealed certain undercurrents—like those waves that can pull a body under.

The question remained: What was the true value of our Casa 4?

Chapter 4 - "Retirement," the Word
Lesson: Know Your Fun Age

Bear with me now for an aside on retirement...since retirement really was an issue lying in wait when we made our purchase. Mister Will's idea to break from the office obviously had been on his mind, just waiting for the right moment to materialize. That moment presented in Mexico like spitting fireworks. Mexico certainly does have an excitement about it that can catch a person off guard. And Mexico certainly attracts many retirees.

It could be that on the 2004 trip, Mister Will really did have in mind more than just breaking from the office...one day. For certain, the word "retirement" was not in *my* everyday vocabulary...unless, of course, referring to someone else. Quite possibly, I had denied this aging-age even to be blinded to the obvious benefits of a more relaxed lifestyle. Once shaken to this phenomenon, I finally caught on: retirement is wonderful.

But that was down the road. First, we needed to find our way. Mister Will needed actually to separate himself from work, little by little, and this plan of his for three months away definitely would send a message to his partners in his then-struggling architectural firm. The headaches that had cropped up were a clue to the need for his cutting back. I already had shorter hours at my paralegal job to facilitate care for my father, who was very frail. The extra time each week did that, but it also offered me a glimpse of life away from a job that did not, and never would, fulfill. I knew without hesitation that I would never want to go back. "Out of here!" was my private thought as I over-enthusiastically waved goodbye to my coworkers as I skipped out the door.

But full retirement wasn't really what we were after at that time—rather, we wanted to *sample* it. Mister Will needed to free himself of worries for a few months each year, also allowing those younger partners to learn the business firsthand. That was his thought. Lucky me, I was along for the ride, hoping secretly for this sort of departure from my legal job. A reason to move on. We were sensing a free and easy turn in our lives. Impetuous comes to mind, if that can be applied to normally cautious people of the Midwest. We agreed that this serendipitous encounter with the seller of Casa 4 could only mean one thing: That our future in Mexico was meant to be! Providence. This was our mindset.

Today, however, all these years later, "free and easy" doesn't necessarily describe me. Better put, I feel free, but not so easy as one might hope. Most days I am pestered even thinking about that word "retirement," like too much chatter in my head. Don't get me wrong—my new newfound freedom with that first Social Security check is something I absolutely do not take for granted. Thank you, Uncle Sam! I am grateful beyond measure.

But it's the stigma of retirement that raises my dander—the notion that in this new category, we seniors are suddenly on the road to decline, diminished in some way. And if my own personal questioning isn't enough, the young technical world out there, for example, gives constant reminders that perhaps I'm out of date, out of step, out of an ancient time that operated much, much slower, if at all. The weight of this negativity is accentuated by what seems like a barrage of force-feeding from the daily media, warning of serious implications for us at that age if not choosing the right foods, activities, sleep habits, medications, and then, this big one...*housing*, appropriate for seniors. Where are we old folks to live, for heaven's sake?

Well, of course, if you ask me, the answer is Mexico! But let's not jump ahead without a fair consideration of other alternatives. Mexico does require a certain hardiness and determination, even for the healthiest and youngest of us travelers. Being realistic, after all, is common wisdom. We can only determine for ourselves how comfortable we will be far, far away from our medical providers at home. Not everyone is up to this.

Take into account too the hardiness and determination that must rise yet above any physical limitations that might come our way. We know those who have done just that. Not just anyone has the muster to take on Mexico after a paralyzing stroke, for instance, or a threatening heart condition, or a severed arm, or blindness, or a shortened limb, or any combination of physical impairments and replaced parts. Not just anyone, that is...except the friends and acquaintances we happen to know who are managing these very conditions of physical challenges I've named, who are perfectly content and happy in Mexico. They wouldn't live their lives in any other way. The term "inspiring" isn't quite enough. So, in Mexico we have these stoic folks who defy the odds when it comes to their health, choosing not to let up despite their physical limitations.

Here at home, assisted living centers promote "every stage of care." Our society seems to be funneling us out of our long-loved, nurturing homes to places not quite so loved or nurturing but with the promise of assistance at every level so that we are sure to take our meds, so that we interact with others, so that we get proper nutrition, so that we don't fall. All this so families can carry on with mom and dad under someone's watchful care. When my own dad as a widower in his late years was hospitalized for a bleeding ulcer after self-medicating with too much aspirin, I recall the stern doctor looking me in the eye with this warning: "People don't live to be old if they live alone!" I cowered.

I quickly and obediently set in motion a different living arrangement for Dad, which meant the only option in his small community: the nursing home. That's quite a jump—from independent living to around-the-clock care—and all because of too much aspirin and not enough housing options for an eighty-eight-year-old in a rural community. But that's what can happen as we circumnavigate the health issues of growing old. And that's how my dad began using a wheelchair when, of course, we all know that a care facility does not want the liability of tottering old folks on the verge of falls. Never mind that nimble Dad could have walked circles around the aides. That's how my dad, energetic and resourceful his entire life no matter the conditions, lived his last six years...in a nursing home. He could have recovered nicely and lived out his elder years in assisted living or even in his own home with assisted support from the county. This alternative is common now and even promoted for the benefit of all. The senior gets to carry on comfortably in his or her own home, and the government gets less of a burden paying costs. But that wasn't an option for my dear dad.

Senior-leaning couples might choose new living arrangements specifically designed for seniors even *before* they have reached retirement and *before* any medical emergencies, just to ensure that their kids aren't left with problems getting old mom and dad out of the house when facing those predictable medical emergencies. But is some of this preplanning going too far? Too scripted? I wonder: Are these couples happy in their new little spaces with their stuff whittled down just because they are "getting up there"? In fact, I do have friends who claim a certain freedom in all that whittling down. More practical than I on such life-changing issues, they simply love the simplicity, and that I understand. But what if that move also brings with it negative thoughts about aging? What if such a move breeds questions on one's self-reliance and purpose? Those negative thoughts, the experts say, make us more likely to develop cardiovascular disease as well as cognitive decline. "Brain aging" they call it.

To be sure, the subject of retirement is complex, without even adding into the mix these nagging health and housing concerns that come with old age. For instance, what does one do with all that extra time? My friend, a retired school principal, has likened the stages of retirement with first grade: Some six-year-olds are ready for school, and some are not. For example, retirement requires a change-up in schedules, activities, maybe even friends. Our scheduled retirement is particular to our set of circumstances, not those of our friends who might happen to work another dozen years. So of course, our social needs are not their social needs anymore. Our life trajectory takes a turn. Apart from that previous life and work style, a beginner in retirement can feel unmoored.

And for those just sailing along into their later years with bodies and homes intact, still there remains the really awful, heavy part of aging: people closest to us dying off. These losses hit hard, take us by surprise, and seem so unfair given this hype our whole lives about the good life after our jobs. "What? We don't get to live long enough to spend at least part of our Social Security benefit?"

What good is this new life if health fails? Just last year alone I counted up another dozen or so contemporaries with serious medical conditions. And with no apparent heads-up, these conditions running the gamut of diseases, just cropped up in their everyday lives after decades of "good health." One minute the freedoms of an able body and the next minute the prison of that same body. "Isn't that the bunk," as my old aunt liked to say. Yes, the bunk. Recently it was a memorial for an old boss who just happened to smoke his whole life—he should have known better, I know, but he did a lot of other things right. He lived his life fully and without regrets, and he laughed a lot, all good. But suddenly, he was stricken, facing an end sooner than he expected. Is that what we're up against? Not knowing? Making choices when we're not sure for how long? Or not deciding anything and waiting it out?

To my thinking, reaching the age of retirement is a two-edged bushwhacking machete. That new status with its benefits of time off and Social Security to boot can be overrated. Held in such high regard for so many of us for decades as we worked long hours, like a finisher's shirt at the end of an endurance race, the retirement package certainly has its drawbacks. It might not fit. Physical challenges and emotional swings seem to pick up just where the workplace paycheck stops. We all know people who finally reach their ultimate goal of retiring only to find themselves empty and wanting. Adrift. Just maybe the psychologists have had it right all along: We need to find our purpose, a new adventure. At least now our society is on to that line of positive thinking. It was Amelia Earhart who said, "Adventure is worthwhile in itself."

To be clumped with all the other retirees in one state of health or another, this category ever-increasing in numbers targeted by every pharmaceutical on the planet...well, it's a burden, to my way of thinking. We want to leave our mark, not squander these precious years. Yet, the weight of more and more losses can sidetrack our best intentions. University of Minnesota Professor Dan Detzner summed up the aging process like this: "Aging is a series of losses." Whoa! That's a bit much. But he explains, it's how we handle those losses...moving on, in other words...that's what makes the difference. From what I can determine, anything to summon up a positive attitude in the midst of a loss is a gift from above.

Help is on the way for this change of attitude if we but look at the condition through a different lens. My friend Shelby, a professional in social sciences, has a useful take on the word "retirement": The term she uses is "re*fire*ment." With the change of just one letter, our new word suddenly conjures up excitement: images of sparks, a burst of energy, a rekindling even. I like that. Nothing there about withdrawing, shrinking from sight, burning out. Nothing about losses. So one might wonder about the possibilities of our later years if, say, Webster himself *retired* the word "retirement" and replaced it with "refirement." A refirement party! Think about it: Our boss might say, "Now that you have worked all these years, you get to be refired!" Charged up for something new, maybe an endeavor you thought had passed, an unachieved goal: that's the thinking behind "refirement." Refired for another go at it. Feel the energy?

Mexico has that verve I'm seeing more and more. Mexico has changed my approach to this stage of life. Maybe it's as simple as the words we use that can shape our attitude. The Spanish language casts a positive spin on retirement, really quite similar to the refirement slant: The word *"jubilacion"* from the Latin *"jubilato"* means rejoicing, originally from the Hebrew *"ubilo."* In the Bible at Leviticus 25:8-13, we read that every 50th year, slaves and prisoners would be set free, debts forgiven, and the mercies of God would be particularly manifest. This was known as the jubilee. Personally, I like the notion that God's mercies would be *particularly* manifest. Like He is mindful that we *particularly* might need His grace at this late time in our lives.

To think of retirement in the Spanish translation, *jubilacion*—that new slant—just might put a skip into our step. We start anew, fresh, having a new lease on life, turning the tables on old and burdened. Free of baggage we have been dragging along, even holding on to for safekeeping, we start anew. Hallelujah for another turn of words... *Jubilacion!*

Spanish has a related term that, at least to my thinking, also casts a more positive slant: *"la tecera edad,"* meaning "the third age." One could argue that this category is not so different from our "senior years," yet, for me at least, a third age feels more open-ended than a senior at the end advancement. I know, this is just a preference for terms, nitpicking really, but maybe the labels we bear define us more than we acknowledge.

Renowned author Isabelle Allende speaks to audiences now about how "to love passionately, no matter your age." Her books reflect this optimism. Maya, the heroin in *Maya's Journal*, admires an elderly but spirited man in the community and writes in her log, "Age, like the clouds, is imprecise and changeable." Whether observing another or evaluating one's own ups and downs with life, we see that the number of our years isn't a reliable measurement for those immeasurable qualities of life, say, joy. The ninety-year-old can be having a more zestful, joyful life than the twenty-year-old.

Studies now find that, in many ways, life does get better as we get older, as in deepened expertise affecting both productivity and creativity and an improved sense of wellbeing with the ability to prioritize what matters most. The findings debunk prevalent aging myths. I personally like to know that Rolling Stone Mick Jagger, now in his late seventies, is still performing after fifty years, and he acknowledges the power of an adrenaline rush. He says, "You can make it work for you." For me, this for sure gets my adrenaline going.

"Happy" is the new condition studied by professors of development and family sciences—specifically, happy with respect to aging. Have you noticed the abundance of self-help books on the subject of happiness? I find it particularly noteworthy that at this time of chaos and anxiety in US politics, that book marketing is focused on personal "happiness." These studies too find that, contrary to long-held beliefs, our happiness doesn't steadily decline as we age but rather, after a high in our twenties, happiness shoots up again after middle age. Imagine that! People in the later years become more relaxed, have more skills for handling challenges, and develop intuitive awareness and insight. My friend, after forty years of working fulltime for a large company said this at her retirement party "It's a wonderful feeling to wake up in the morning and know each day going forward is my own! I'm happy!"

So, what if this mindset of happy and improved well-being were to replace the mindset of age-related medical concerns? What if we turn off the pharmaceutical ads and tune out the naysayers? Let's cram our minds with all positive and leave no room for the negative. Let's throw our bags in the car and get ready for adventure! What if *refirement* is what we are aiming for after all?

Mexico has been my adventure, my refirement. The rugged spaces, the ancient history, the Mexican people so different, yet so very much like ourselves. These are the pieces of my third age, my age of *jubilacion*. The music calls.

Chapter 5 – Our Condo Family
Lesson: Know the Back Story

Back to those undercurrents awaiting us at our new home away from home, our dream come true—we had a lot to learn. You with an eye on Mexican property, take note. Quite possibly, Mr. Will and I could have benefited from pointed questions to the seller about specifics of this condo association we were buying into. We should have asked exactly who owed what and, more specifically, was everyone paid up. The truth is, the notion that an owner might be delinquent in paying the annual fees did not enter our minds. Who with any pride in ownership would own such a piece of valuable real estate and fail to stay current with the reasonable annual fees? Or, the notion that the association's bank account might be lacking. Aren't budgets meant to be followed? Or this: That some owners might rent their units willy-nilly to just anyone off the street? Don't all owners cherish their Mexican getaway, like a beloved home away from home? Indeed, Mr. Will and I only saw the glossy cover.

The cast of characters over the years at our new little getaway speaks volumes about how we might not always see eye to eye with our co-owners. Condo life by nature means a certain loss of privacy, especially so in the open-air environment of warm weather living. Windows are open, voices carry. What might be seen as nosiness or even spying on one another is simply the effect of a close living arrangement. We see who is coming and who is going. And with our different backgrounds, languages, and cultures, we tend to wonder and speculate a little too much about what each other is up to. One guest put it this way: "It's a little like Peyton Place."

We do, of course, have common property in this condo setup, so it follows that rules about the common areas must be followed to accommodate all. Now then, how we each interpret those rules gets tricky. The language barrier isn't always the main hurdle. Posada del Sol, our ten-unit condominium group, does have more Mexican owners: six to our four from the US and Canada. One can't deny that speaking the same language most certainly is a plus when, say, negotiating a business deal. But honestly, even those whose native tongue is English—that would be us from the US and Canada—we are often worlds apart. One might think that those of us from *el norte* might be more unified just with language alone, but human nature being what it is—and, honestly, condo nature being what it is—we sometimes miss the point of fellowship in our little vacation haven.

Maybe it's just that twisted Posada history I alluded to that somehow attracted yet more twisted customers. Here I will briefly describe, as an example, the makeup of our little association, which frankly is not much off the norm for condos in

Mexico. You potential buyers, take note. This is the type of detail that might raise a red flag if negotiating a purchase...or give the go-ahead...but at least it's front and center of the deal.

Those folks I will single out here, both North Americans and Mexicans, are those we have always understood to be the core group at Posada. They set the beat. Then after a couple of decades to this beat, Mister Will and I came along without a clue and slightly out of step. We were in effect dropped into a North American square dance set to a Mexican rhythm.

Let me be clear from what I have learned so far: any Mexican condo association out there—not just ours—has its share of angst among the owners, whether it's about delinquent payments or no payments at all. Or, as to general unrest no matter the culture, look no further than an owner obsessed with tidiness and strict rules to bring it out in those more concerned with overall compatibility in the cross-cultural group. No one is perfect, but come on, you want to say, let's get along— - this is Mexico.

Let me begin this twisted history: To be fair, I'll start this summary of characters with us. Certainly, Mister Will and I have the distinction of most gullible, nicey-nicies, idealistic to the core. Can't help it. Was it the years of church work decades ago that gave us a bad name? The notion that Posada might have some shady secrets or at the very least, a troublesome bank account, didn't cross our minds. After all, the seller we were dealing with was another one of us from *el norte*, even our home state of Minnesota. So, we trust a lot. We exercise, eat right, drink usually not too much. Wild parties are not for us...but we do like to party, give us that.

Next up is this seller - I'll call her Super Gal - who, on the one hand, seemed a lot like us - hard-working Minnesotan and all - but on the other hand, had her own agenda to sell. That agenda, so driven by another Posada long-timer, necessarily meant withholding certain condo information from us wide-eyed Minnesota prospects in order to clinch a deal...certain heavy duty condo information as in an enormous water bill in arrears for five-plus years, an enormous Federal Zone tax in arrears for ten-plus years, information of that nature. Then too, Super Gal withheld her personal story involving an incident with a Molotov cocktail which occurred on our street directly in front of our gate. Not that this random incident might sway our ultimate decision to buy, but Super Gal must have thought so, extra secretive as she was about any Mexico dangers whatsoever when trying to snag a buyer. We understand that thinking now. The incident, we eventually learned, did involve a robbery at our supermarket and a high-speed chase down our boulevard, with the car bomb tactic only to detract police. The car bomb just happened to land in Super Gal's Honda Sierra parked at Posada del Sol. That can occur anywhere, right?

So the particulars of this subject property weren't entirely laid out to us. And the fact that certain information was withheld, well, we could only wonder. What else might she be withholding? It would be a year later, at our condo annual meeting, that we would first learn about the enormous unpaid water bill and the enormous unpaid Federal Zone bill, now part of our responsibility as owners. "We owe how much...for debts before our time here? Really?" Okay, we're partly to blame for total trust in mankind and especially as to fellow-Minnesotans. We are adults and know the basic caution: "buyer beware." Let me say again because this can't be overstated: Shouldn't we have asked specific questions about this condo organization? Of course. Or, how about some leading questions like: "Are any of the owners in arrears? Does the association have any outstanding bills? Do the owners get along? What exactly are the Mexican laws on such issues?"

Our seller Super Gal, a tough woman in every aspect, even to drive to Mexico on her own as a sixty-something widow - remember, that's 2,300 miles one way, crossing an international border, by herself - taught us our first lesson at Posada: beware of double identities. With eye-popping surprise we stumbled across revealing nude photos left tucked in a closet and learned that Mexico is a hot spot for plastic surgeries. That marked the day when Mister Will and I began to wonder seriously about our own intentions and, frankly, the intentions of other foreigners like ourselves living in Mexico: Perhaps Mexico *is* a place to escape; perhaps Mexico does bring out another side to ourselves; perhaps, especially in Mexico, none of this matters.

    The other Posada long-timer also was from here in the Midwest. Stories abound on how this long-timer—I'll call her Queen Bee—and her husband in fact were the first purchasers of the place in the sixties. Queen Bee literally ran Posada and orchestrated the selling of various units those first years to folks from the US, again, the Midwest in fact. Then, we're told, some thirty years later, Queen Bee sold her prime unit on the beach to a wealthy Mexican businessman. That sale apparently was the impetus for Super Gal's less-than-forthright dealings with us. After all, so the gossip goes, if Queen Bee could get that much for hers, then Super Gal could too. Set two competitive women in motion, and you witness power. That particular wealthy Mexican businessman—I'll call him The *Don*—would eventually change the Posada landscape, literally...again with improprieties. It was a recent summer while we Americanos and Canadians were back home, when The *Don* maneuvered the covert construction of a second story to his condo, absolutely and unequivocally against condo rules, or at least the rules as we understood them. Surprise! This blatant disregard for our association regulations obviously caused a certain divide—more like chasm—

between the owners. The Mexicans, we've come to learn, more or less accept such roguish behavior, while we from *el norte* more or less like to obey the rules to the tee. "It's not fair!" we whined. Some of us, take our Casa 4 for example, have been affected by less sea breeze with that second story blocking some of our ocean air. Shade on our pool has increased. These are no small matters when it comes to tropical vacations. But no amount of groveling has helped—in fact, now two of the other Mexican owners have petitioned for their own second floors.

Years before Queen Bee sold her unit to The *Don*, she had already taken under her wing another Mexican, this the first ever Mexicano to own at Posada. Quite a deviation from all North American folks, oh dear. Now decades later, even the retelling of that piece of Posada history sets off gnashing of teeth among the current gringo owners. Up until that sale, the owners were either Americano or Canadian, in other words, all spoke English, and, from our understanding, all respected the obligations of paying their fees on time and all followed rules. This Mexicano prospect was slick talking with a questionable background and no money: I'll call him Smooth Talker. Still unclear on the details, and I certainly don't want to misrepresent in any way, but this is what we hear: Apparently a still-unresolved sales transaction with a Canadian, now missing, got Smooth Talker his condo at Posada. Smooth Talker and his family haven't budged in all these decades. Here I must be clear that it is not his family we have an issue with—Smooth Talker's wife is very pleasant and hardworking, a lovely person, really, and likely does not know the full scope of her husband's business dealings. We, being co-owners, just want fair play.

For several years, the sleezy bar just across the street was operated by Smooth Talker, then was rented out to another low-life organization, and now sits empty. Thanks for that. But during those years, Smooth Talker's young employees frequenting our grounds on a regular basis year after year, for whatever reason even if just coming to get paid, only stoked our imaginations with images of, say, drug deals. I mean, gosh...our minds can easily go on overdrive when money is due in a country where, word has it, drug deals run rampant in everyday businesses. Lest I say, we are always on our toes. That still-unresolved transaction from way back when with the now-missing Canadian, we have learned, was the undoing of Posada...that is to say, the original Posada owned by Americanos and Canadians. And *that* transaction is how Posada got into debt.

The coming and going of the various owners after that first ownership by a Mexican gets a little fuzzy for me except I know that the group from the States back in the eighties liked to party and hang out as a group. Several of those owners were the result of Queen Bee's initial teaming of owners from the US. Picture several forty-something couples from the Midwest living the good life for a few short weeks every winter on the coast of Mexico. One downside lingers, however: Sales transactions and property ownership rights, which were perfectly legitimate in the States, have yet to pass the convoluted test in Mexico. For at least one of those condo units, the question remains to this day: Whose name is on that title anyway?

Just to deviate slightly for the sake of thoroughness, that group mentality I described still pervades many a beach condo organization, whether the residents are owners or renters. "Herd mentality" is the term used by some who chafe at the notion of mind-numbing group activities. A potluck every Friday? Are you in or not? That question always lingers. So, consider your tolerances.

But about our condo history: At Posada, the ownership by Mexicanos, after Smooth Talker broke the code, evolved over the years, much to the dismay of the folks from *el norte*. What I've learned in talking with acquaintances familiar to Mexican condo living—and Mexicanos themselves will tell you this—it is considered fact that Mexicanos tend *not* to pay in a timely manner...though they do eventually pay. This of course is counter to everything we gringos have learned since high school business class. Fearing a bad credit rating, exponential interest, or at the very least a sorry reputation, I learned to pay my bills on time, and even early.

Another example: One of the problematic Mexican payers whom we never had the occasion to meet, owned a small ice cream shop in downtown Manzanillo. I'll call him Ice Cream Man. His condo was always available to rent, so we at Posada met various renters over the years. Never once did we actually see the elusive Ice Cream Man. Convenient for him, his employee at the shop took care of the Posada books. You notice I use the words "took care of" rather than a more business term like "managed." Never once in her Posada duties did she present to the owners an actual written report of the finances; she preferred to show up at our meetings with only an unruly stack of receipts and call it done. Even in a common language, one must agree that this simply does not add up. With our paltry Spanish to top it off, we from *el norte* were destined never to know where our money went. Quite possibly the ice cream shop? This setup carried on for years, and then by the grace of God, an upstanding Mexican couple arrived a few years ago as the new owners of that famed unit. The ice cream shop, we hear, is still going strong.

Another Mexican owner, a respected eye doctor—in fact, I'll call him The Doc—makes his annual payment only after repeated requests, and then threats, by the condo president. On and on it goes each year. The Doc fills his condo to the brim with family and extended family, pouring into the common spaces and even onto private patios when those owners are absent—once, we're told, using our patio while we were back in Minnesota to park his refrigerator during a remodel project. No harm, but still. Gregarious and flamboyant, The Doc is like the rich kid in class who always acts up. Like a game for him, he waits until all are at attention with the suspense...then pays with a laugh, smoothing differences with gifts. A bottle of wine perhaps? The problem is that he and his family are so likable.

The Mexicano family who seem to anchor Posada del Sol, and do make their payments on a timely basis, more or less, own two of the units, one of which by the family matriarch, now recently deceased at age 94. That unit has since been carried on by siblings. The other family unit is owned by a daughter and her husband, a reputable contractor from Guadalajara. I'll call them The Family. Owning numerous Mexican properties, including a tequila ranch, The Family has a respectable presence. Under this leadership, Posada began to see the light of day...but not without suspicion: Ne'r-do-well Smooth Talker continues to shake a finger about misallocation of money in those years. The overpriced wall between Posada and the public access, he continues to point out, is just one example of bad faith—quite possibly that expensive wall was in exchange for business favors? When, as a reaction to that nonsense and in defense for that Posada leadership, Mister Will blurted, "That's a bunch of crap!" Smooth Talker revealed his still darker side with a nasty threat in plain English: "You know I could put drugs in your car at any time..."

Really? How does one even respond to that? Well, I have to say flat out that the comment shocked us, even to conjure up a bit of fear. That was the first and only time the word "drugs" has been used in the context of us and our wellbeing...like our safety could be in jeopardy crossing the border with drugs planted in our car? Us? With that threat, even if just off-hand intimidation, Mister Will knew best to shut up and say no more. I like that about Mister Will—his coolness. I might have....well...I'm not sure, but I can picture myself throwing out ugly names, marching off to talk to Smooth Talker's wife at the very least. But then, as I said, she likely would know nothing about her husband's business dealings or connections. The country of Mexico is highly male-dominated.

As it turns out, since that confrontation, no altercations, no scuffles. Mister Will and I mind our own business, and the relationship stays on an even keel, as if the conversation didn't happen. All of us now are politely civil with our greetings whenever we cross paths. *"Buenos dias. Como esta?"* And, to be open-minded and honest here, Mister Will and I do acknowledge that certain kindnesses have been shown to us by Smooth Talker from time to time. He even served up margaritas at Mister Will's birthday party. Now after years really, analyzing those threatening words from every angle, I suspect that Smooth Talker was just playing into our foreign jitters on such topics to keep us off balance, that sort of psychological play. But that would be dark humor, if you ask me.

Nevertheless, between the Mexican owners themselves, accusations still simmer. A fistfight over a misplaced patio table one recent year sent Smooth Talker and his "thugs," as I refer to them, to jail. A turf war! We watch and wait for the court's decision, but Mister Will and I bet that Smooth Talker will talk his way through this too.

This spicy, medium-hot, rundown of characters is our Posada del Sol, our dream come true, our winter getaway that just so happens to have a tangled backstory, tales of shenanigans, and a history of crisis management. This is our dear Mexican home. Caveat: As with the nature of group living, some of this information is firsthand and some is pure gossip, for which I apologize. But, how can I be discreet yet forthright in my duty to write what I'm living in Mexican-style condo world?

With this set of characters as backdrop, let me say that Posada has evolved from the button-down gringo group who were there at the beginning into a saucy *grupo mixta Mexicano-gringo*. Dare I even mention that these seemingly less-than-forthright doings by our Mexican neighbors, the late payments, and so on as described, are somehow easier to accept than perhaps a few social disconnects with our neighbors from *el norte*? That's right: Often it's our own U.S. and Canadian neighbors that cause fits. That's how it is sometimes when the heat gets to you - the littlest thing can get under your skin. Such disconnects run the gambit of un-neighborly considerations when sharing common property, from the rule-of-law restrictions on laundry facilities to the proper and timely locking and unlocking of the front gate. And these are some of the finest people I know, all honest, hardworking, smart people, and frankly, with a good sense of humor. But obviously we do have our different lifestyles and personalities and do get misdirected in staking our respective claims.

Irrespective of our cultural differences, I fault our tight, open-air living spaces for any disconnects. We know entirely too much about each other's whereabouts at all times - our business becomes their business, and visa- versa. Too much information. I have often joked that our neighbors know precisely when our toast pops up in the morning. For certain, what with the building configuration featuring our condos clustered around the pool, we all are alert to the any comings and goings through our front gate. "Exactly who is visiting them now?" is an incessant preoccupation.

And, I fault the loose Mexicano condo rules which, to our detriment, none of us gringos can pin down exactly...so we guess. Lacking adequate language skills, we from *el norte* are consumed with speculation about our Mexicano owners. Condo issues such as late payments, excessive guests, and loud music at the pool, to name a few, are the topics we hash among ourselves over our afternoon *cervezas* and game of dominos. This type of group deduction mostly stirs up inaccurate information, or at least questionable third-hand information.

Valid hearsay is tough enough without the extra hurdle of language barrier. For example, say one of us owners sides up with one of the Mexicanos on any particular dispute and then it turns out, after an accurate translation that the information was all wrong. You see how the *tortilla* soup thickens. That inaccurate information leads to finger-pointing, which in turn leads to gossip.

If not careful to be rational, we gringos are destined to be at each other's throats for no reason at all except a miscue. An incessant churning of the rumor mill hasn't helped in this regard. "What the hell is safe to say and what isn't?..." I ask Mister Will in a feverish pitch. "...and in which language?"

Then there's this other touchy issue of cross-cultural good form: When trying to tip-toe ever so politely between the two cultures, as Mister Will and I were trained thoroughly in those early years working at the hacienda mission with the Mazahuan people, we personally find it extremely unsettling if one of us from *el norte* misbehaves. Such brazen behavior was oh so evident in the indiscriminate axing of a new palm tree on the beach to save the view. Yee, gads! That makes all of us gringos look bad—that lowers us to the label "Ugly American," pushing our own ethnocentric agenda. That particular instance, arousing such anger as to chop down a palm tree in the middle of the night, comes down to a distinct cultural difference: Mexicanos love their *palmas,* the more the better; the rest of us, well, not if the damned *palmas* shade the pool or block the ocean view. Alas, it's this ocean detail that binds us and separates us.

We owners, each of us, do strive to get along in our little condo community, really we do. That's obvious in the gestures of goodwill after tempers cool down, as simple as handing out extra berries from the market or sharing a family story from home. And aren't these petty grievances the baggage of most condo groups, no matter the country or culture? If not palm trees, then something else, right? Close living conditions require work. Indiscriminate *something* tends to happen in condo groups; that's how Mister Will and I have learned to see it.

Those social disconnects aside, we US and Canadian owners do claim a strong bond. We are foreigners, the visitors to this very different culture in Mexico. So by definition, we must adhere to our own set of rules at least for peace of mind. And we do have a bit of longevity at Posada. Staying power, I say. Casa 1 has been in the same family for two generations, that's nearly a whopping fifty years. The adventuresome and fearless couple back in seventies—making the trip from Iowa by car, mind you—were pioneers in their own right. Who wouldn't predict that their kids who were hauled along all those years also would develop a deep affection for Mexico? Our friends—that second generation, and a third coming up—are hell-bound for Manzanillo every year. Steeped in the history and traditions of long-ago Manzanillo, they never fail to come up with a good story, straight out of wild-west Mexico, as in, "Did you ever hear about the pool maintenance guy who was electrocuted down in that pool pit and all the gringos fled, fearing the Mexican courts?" "Yes!" we say, "But do tell it again," as we reach for another Modelo. Or, looking for more drama, we egg on, "How about that big earthquake back in the eighties when the boulevard was all busted up...tell us about that!"

The owner of Casa 5 has been a long-timer too. But that story, sad to report, is one about improper ownership papers decades ago between two parties, both from the US. A thicket of Mexican law stands between Owner Casa 5 and clear title. Meanwhile, she, now a widow, maintains her condo requirements and has enjoyed a visit each year until recently. Now we other owners speculate: "Does she plan to sell? But how can she sell without the proper papers? And what sort of work needs to be done to Casa 5 after sitting idle for so long...the dirt...can you imagine the dirt?" This is the fodder for our routine murmurings.

Casa 10, the only one-bedroom condo at Posada—really more like an efficiency—was owned by a Canadian couple for at least fifteen years. Stories go that this was housing for Posada's security and maintenance guy, back in the hay days when Posada enjoyed not only around-the-clock security but also maid service twice a week. This couple from British Columbia, looking for a touch of hot weather, landed a good deal with this tiny place. They have the distinction of driving the farthest: Oh my...well over 3,000 miles. That's a seven-day trip one way! These Canadians owning Casa 10 adored the heat and everything spicy and loud and wild and reckless about Mexico. And the tiny accommodations? They packed in with gusto whoever visited. Sadly, poor health put an end to their stays in Mexico. A new owner (this time US) has the place now and is equally as joyful about owning this little piece of the Pacific. And, as you might guess, the new owner is family of Casa 1.

This much can be said about our really old, low-profile, *mostly* one story, and relatively cheap Posada: It doesn't weigh on the conscience quite like, say, a glitzy new high-end model just out on the market, complete with marble countertops and an infinity pool—now *that* would be talking big dollars. So, in that line of thinking, if our casa at Posada sits idle for a year or two, any downside is not going to break the pocketbook. It's all about risks. Think about your own financial cushion.

Personally, for Mister Will and myself, when we drive away from Posada each spring, any of the aforementioned condo worries and drama fade with the miles as we speed north. Our Casa 4 is "buttoned down," we say. Furniture is draped with sheets; wall hangings, kitchen appliances, anything not nailed down is tucked away; patio furniture is stored inside—as if carefully packed and stored for nine months in Mex-Storage. We rely on good fortune that Casa 4 will be there for us when we return. By the time we cross back from Mexico into the States, our thoughts have turned to our home in Minnesota. We owners at Posada rest easy. Still, we wonder and continue to rehash: So what about that Casa 5 and its tangled web of ownership? What about that?

The various renters over the years really don't fit in this category "Our Condo Family" except possibly a Canadian couple who continued to rent for more than a dozen years from The Family, that's Casa 3. Twelve not-always-smooth years. No matter the sometimes-questionable rental conditions that presented over that time, as in leaky pipes, ant infestations, a sluggish toilet, and overflowing sewage, these two stuck it out. To their credit, this couple added kitchen conveniences here and there and even spiffed up where they saw a need, as in decent reading lamps and upgraded patio chairs. They purchased a gas grill. They even went so far as to pay for television repair, roof repair, and window security. Like gifts for The Family, these upgrades most definitely ensured a good relationship between owner and renter for many years. Take note, you renters out there.

"They act like they own the place!" we owners observed about these renters from the sidelines of our patios. Then, wagging fingers, we added among ourselves, "Well not really like owning." Smug in our unique role as actual owners of Mexican property and all its snags, we wanted to say: "How about you smart-talking renters maintain the place and pay the yearly dues and taxes, sit through those dreaded meetings, navigate the Spanish language and Mexican culture for acceptable condo management, and let's not forget, have legitimate papers on your place, pay the fifty-year trust...only then can you begin to experience ownership in Mexico." That's been the consensus among us. Still, the two were tenacious and fought like hell to maintain status quo with those of us owning at Posada. Must I say, they won us over. And now, the widow continues to carry on at Posada, but with her canine companion. Such is the call to Mexico.

But hold on...one more player in this condo family needs mention. He doesn't own a unit or even live at Posada, but he loves and embraces Posada like his own home. It's Roque. He is our hardworking groundskeeper, maintenance man, and all-around get-things-done guy, who has had Posada under his wing for eighteen years now, beginning this career when he was just twenty something. Longevity like that at any Mexican condo is rare. So we owners adore him. Not that he hasn't given us pause a few times, siding with this or that faction when Posada has struggled with leadership, but Roque has proven his loyalty time and time again. He likely has been the glue holding us owners together through the ups and downs at our Posada. If I were to imagine a great storyline about Posada another twenty years from now, I might picture Roque as a proud owner himself and even cashing in on a very lucrative rental market to folks from *el norte*. He, of course, would be addressed as *"Senor Roque,"* and a young maintenance worker would be fetching water for him.

Chapter 6 - *Tiempo*
Lesson: Know How Much You Like Your Watch

The following musing is an entry from my Manzanillo journal when I contemplated a particular day's priorities and how differently time itself is viewed in our cultures:

> "What a strange place this is: Painting has been on our minds, just like every year when we arrive at Posada. Fresh white paint on the exterior of our condos makes all seem brand new. The harsh ocean climate in this industrial port city wears heavily on buildings, leaving dirt and chipped paint. A yearly painting is a must. But when is this painting a priority? We from the north expect it now, today, soon—to the local Mexicans, it's the

famous "*mañana.*" We wait, we inquire, we wait.

"Today, as we continued to wait, our maintenance worker Roque with an obvious deep sense of pride in his culture painted the trunks of our palm trees. For him, the *palmas* had priority, not our condos."

And so we learn to wait and eventually welcome the difference.

Rather than a daily medication for, say, easing one's stress, perhaps a doctor might prescribe a lengthy stay in Mexico—and it just might work. The prescription might read: Unstructured activities of one's own choosing, as-needed basis, unlimited, guided only by the sun. Side effects: whimsical wanderings, relinquishment of time pieces lackadaisical attention to US politics and things of that sort."

As one might expect, no matter where, when any of us North Americans vacation and are away from our jobs and family responsibilities—and certainly in retirement—we experience this thing of extra time. But the luxury of those hours sometimes falls flat with our wound-up psyches still marching to our clocks. Even in retirement mode at our home in Minnesota, we continue the micro scheduling of our days, and we mark our time by measuring accomplishments, big and small, as in checking off our to-do lists, even our "bucket lists." That mentality is so deep in our DNA that our trying really hard to let loose can have an unintended opposite effect...wound up. Change has its own stress. Somehow the stress of our self-made timetables is often more comfortable than to completely let go, so those first days in Mexico, we innocently continue keeping pace to our clocks...expecting the unreasonable from a culture that has its own rhythm, a rhythm not based on clocks. Perhaps, I wonder, it's a rhythm based on Spanish music of the centuries? The Spanish word for time in fact is *tiempo,* not so much different from our English "tempo" which, of course, is the speed of a musical piece. But we from the north keep in step with our ticking clocks. And then one day, as if suddenly awakened to a novel idea, we feel that new rhythm in our being, as if swaying to a *bolero,* and we leave our watches behind. Mexico simply doesn't acknowledge timetables.

Mister Will and I catch ourselves slipping back into old habits from the north, but now, many years into this, we're catching on to this wonder of "Mexican time." On any given day while we are in Manzanillo, our good intentions may shift with the prevailing winds or simply evaporate in the heat of day...and here's the best part: We don't care. We surrender to our body rhythms. Friends stop by on the spot, and we eagerly grab a chair and a drink to catch up. Or our moods might change the plan. Our to-do list—yes, I still have the habit—is suddenly put off for the next day. *Mañana.*

Many of our daily talking points as we meet up with our friends are about exactly this issue of scheduling-gone-mad...the repairman who hasn't shown up, the upholstery job that is overdue, the condo meeting that didn't happen, the cable connection that we hope will happen soon...and we share laughs. The bonding factor on this phenomenon alone is powerful. We can always connect with someone who has a story similar to ours, or even more outrageous. We've learned that in Mexico, we too can put off until *mañana.* How much better, we have learned, to accept it and, one step further, *to experience* some of that latitude ourselves. It's the relationships that matter, not the schedules, not the clock: This is our new watchword: *mañana.*

In Mexico, the sun is our clock, as it should be, the sleep experts say. But more than the effect of our bodies' circadian rhythms when it comes to sleep patterns, the southern sun guides our activities throughout the day. Warm...very warm...hot! Even in our northern home situated at 45 degrees parallel, we know the sun effect, but there, our concern might be just when to add a jacket.

Our Manzanillo sun defies the image of blazing Mexico heat in the gentle, glorious presence it makes each morning as it crests the horizon. Cast against the mountains and the ocean, it frames the day in cool pastels. Give it, say, an hour, however, and those colors quickly turn intense. We exercise-sorts are wise to hit the track by seven or eight o'clock, certainly no later than nine, which is pushing heat tolerance while challenging our bodies during aerobic and anaerobic workouts. Now many years into this experience, we are more accustomed to the heat and, as couch psychologists say, "embrace it." I like to imagine that the morning sun exposure is perhaps even healthy, as in a daily supply of Vitamin D, although my dermatologist would argue mightily. Even the locals at the track seem to duck out from the direct sun by mid-morning. Mister Will and I wear our caps.

The morning workout program comes naturally to us after so many years at our Minnesota YMCA. But dedicating our mornings not only to exercise but including a leisurely breakfast routine does go against the norm in Mexico because our priorities in that way of course eliminate any shopping or errands before the heat of the day. Small price to pay, we say, for easing into the day our style. Yet, we want to participate in all things Mexican.

This heat survival concept is wired into the locals. The markets are abuzz each morning, with shop owners staying one step ahead of the eager buyers lined up, *pesos* exchanging for *bolsas* of fruits, vegetables, fresh cuts of meat, catches of the day, still-warm-from-the-grill *tortillas*. The crusty local bread, *pan bolillo* is pedaled fresh from a vendor on the street with a catchy jingle blaring from his scooter. By noon, the crowds diminish, and by two o'clock, the shop owners can be caught half napping in their stalls.

This naturally brings me to *siesta,* which, time and time again, is precisely when Mister Will and I begin our shopping. This has become our private joke. Let's face it: We are out of sync. The best we seem to do, holding true to our preferred morning routine, is to hold off our shopping until just after the *siesta,* although that's not a good option either because by then the produce is picked over or gone altogether. Or, we shop at the big stores and the supermarkets which do not abide by the *siesta* rule. We aren't proud of this. It's not the old Mexican way and certainly doesn't help the small business guy, we know, but we do accomplish our shopping. To feel better about our habits of trade, we do shop at the weekly market where locals bring their goods. You see the dilemma.

But the concept we get. My Spanish dictionary says this about *siesta*: "hottest time of the day; afternoon nap." The two go hand in hand, illustrated by the stereotypical *sombrero*-wearing fellow dozing in the shade of a cactus under the hot sun. Are your eyelids becoming heavy? Find a hammock, a piece of shade, grab a book, or just close your eyes and wait while the heat sizzles. And wait for the shops to open again.

A recent year when we replaced our windows at Casa 4, the workers had their "noon break," as we from the north call it, during that hottest time of the day, at the two to three o'clock period in the afternoon, sometimes later. Then they returned to work and didn't quit for the day until seven o'clock. This seems to be the standard work schedule too for most of the local small businesses and vendor stalls: by late afternoon, activities resume until early evening.

While we wait, the locals rest, and then they enjoy their big meal of the day, *la comida,* which is often around two o'clock. A fair number of the traditional Mexican restaurants cater to this afternoon meal, and especially on weekends, they even entertain with a *mariachi* band. Often about that time in mid-afternoon, I have stopped in my tracks at the first notes of trumpets and guitars as they tune their instruments in the nearby restaurant. Ah, yes, I remind myself with a smile, it's *mariachi* time at El Bigotes. With the prevailing breezes blowing in our favor at Casa 4, Mister Will and I find ourselves humming along and tapping our toes with the dance rhythms.

We the foreigners, the visitors in this very different lifestyle, take note. Even at home in the US, we see that those who nap are suddenly gaining respect, not only from physicians who claim health benefits but from employers who see monetary benefits in rested employees. Some of our friends seem to have caught on better than we have with the Mexican way. But even for Mister Will and myself, slightly rigid with our northern routines, the lesson of the *siesta* is settling in. A little doze in the shade or under a fan while the temperature peaks refreshes like nothing else for another go at activities in late afternoon.

Taking time to observe a sunset literally anywhere in the world, with or without obstructions to the horizon, is nothing less than a humbling tribute to the work of a higher power—an acceptance of another day's end. But to experience a sunset over an ocean—to actually see the sun as it "sits" on the ocean's edge and then slips away—is profoundly inspiring and magical. That must explain why Mister Will and I have literally dozens of sunset photographs. Whether it's a shot of the sun as it's perched on the water, or the sun framing a ship in the far distance, or the sun over the peninsula at its farthest point to the north, which happens to signal our return home...all of those plus seemingly limitless variations, we have those.

And it's not just the foreigners vacationing like ourselves who get into this sunset routine. The locals gather for this photo op too, even workers still in uniform from their jobs. As the day winds down and the sun is low in the sky, these spectators of all varieties start arriving at the beach armed with beach chairs, blankets, refreshments, children, and dogs in tow...and with cameras. Especially in today's world of cell phone technology, nearly everyone has an opportunity to record an event: this, a winsome photo of *puesta del sol*. Taking in the majesty of a sunset, as with any wonder of nature, seems to be another one of those human expressions common across cultures, as is music and the arts, where we can truly relate to each other, no matter the language barrier. So it is for us in Mexico, each evening when our cultures mix with one priority: the sunset.

An ocean sunset is also why we, from *el norte* at least, never fail to watch for "the green flash," as the atmospheric phenomenon is known by those of us who consider ourselves experts on the subject. Apparently, under precise conditions, a green shooting aura is cast at the second the sun dips below the horizon. Those watching for it dare not blink. Well, I will attest to seeing some version of that anyway, or maybe that year of 2008 it was the effect of a second Modelo mixed with the pleasures of an exotic ocean breeze and a bigger-than-life Panavision sky...but then, that might be a phenomenon too.

Contrary to logic, a cloudy day sometimes lands the best sunset visuals. Either the clouds shift at the last moment as if opening a tiny window or two so the sun peeks through on its way to the horizon, here, then there, or the bank of clouds at the horizon lift like a shade to reveal a thin last look at the sun setting over the water. Or maybe the clouds hide the sunset entirely, but wait...the show is about to begin. The after-effects of a sunset are often stunning, a show unto itself as those sun rays beaming up from the horizon arc across the sky to backlight the clouds, spotlighting the stratosphere, bouncing here then there in blues and yellows and pinks and mangos. We sit at the seawall, heads bobbing one direction to another as we discover a new dramatic highlight in the expanse of sky. Ohhh.

A particular bliss settled upon me one evening before sunset when music from the beach drew me to the wall to have a look. There on the beach was a gathering, which I recognized as one of our large Mexican families, under an oversized umbrella enjoying food and drinks, with children darting in and around playing in the sand, all obviously enjoying themselves. This was Good Friday, that part of Holy Week, *Semana Santa,* when crowds converge on Mexico's coastal cities for a long holiday. That's the week of the year that we foreigners try to avoid in our getaway plans. Crowds. But, as Mister Will and I have learned, crowds in Mexico sometimes enlighten us and broaden our perspective. Sometimes we feel as one.

This Mexican family was being serenaded by a mariachi band. The twelve musicians there on the beach in full *charro* dress held nothing back as they played tune after tune, face-to-face with their adoring audience. The family laughed, they danced, they snuggled when the rhythms turned romantic and the sun was at the horizon. From the sea wall where we sat, Mister Will and I, the spectators, toasted with our *cervesas*— and time stood still.

Chapter 7 - Owning, Part I
Lesson: Know How Much You Like Your Stuff

Note: Unless you have a nagging curiosity about buying Mexican property yourself (and you scored high on my list from Chapter 1) or you want to understand the quirks of someone who actually owns Mexican property, you might prefer to skip the next three chapters. Owning is a rite onto itself which, I believe, is worth noting in the categories I have set out, roughly: your stuff, your neighbors, your community. Look at it like a study in avoiding ownership pitfalls. Regardless, you might just be intrigued enough to read everything you get your hands on to more fully understand our neighbors south of the border. Look at it like a study in building bridges.

Trust the Trust

Condo living was new to us when we signed up for our Casa 4, so right off the bat we had a big change of living ahead of us: no more single-family dwelling for these three months. But that didn't get our attention really; we were focused instead on the complexities of doing the deal, obtaining title to beach property in Mexico, maneuvering the legalities, making it ours. We had heard variations of this difficult process, the worries, the frustrations, and worst of all the deals that didn't happen. Ours was relatively easy.

It's true that compared to a normal real estate transaction back home, owning beach property in Mexico as a foreigner requires a bit of doing, to put it mildly, with even an extra hurdle: the land trust. Here's the deal: It's not like we own the land. That's the thing in Mexico. Any land within fifty kilometers (31 miles) of the coast or 100 kilometers (62 miles) of an international border cannot be owned by a foreigner, only the building on that land—in other words, anything above ground. "That's crazy!" you say.

Well, that giant extra hurdle is a formidable enough barrier for many foreigners that they back down and take an easier route for spending time in Mexico: rentals. Easy. Many of our friends do just that for their two- or three-month stay. Their worries are few beyond coming up with the cash deposit for the rental, of course, and accepting the inevitable vagaries with rentals in a far away foreign country, as in where and how to make that rental deposit in pesos or dollars, how to be confident about the condition of the rental premises as understood, and how best to communicate long distance in the interim...email, phone, nothing? And what if plans change? Communicating these terms in two languages is at best confusing. Here again is where total reliance and flexibility go a long way: reliance that the habitation is still under that ownership and still yours on that set date many months ahead and flexibility to handle whatever the situation is when you arrive.

The friends we know who rent routinely sign up when they leave each spring, and they communicate mid-year by email to assure the reservation. Mexican management is getting wise to the idea that North Americans set high standards but with big pocketbooks, plus North Americans are easy on the premises in their tidiness. Welcome, amigos from the US and Canada! The Mexican owners even offer storage areas for the North Americans to hold some of their goods for the next year. One downside to scheduling, however: Prime time is off limits. That is, Easter rentals are reserved for the masses of *Mexicanos* who come to the coast for the holiday; they pay a higher fee. Noticeably then, a week before Easter, the North Americans suddenly are absent.

Nowadays, with online vacation rentals so prevalent, the process has become a whole lot easier. However, beware those of you using that online service! We know firsthand of honest, well-meaning renters who were kicked out of a Mexican condo because the bona fide owner was unaware of the deal and, frankly, didn't offer the condo for rental in the first place. How's that for quick *dinero* in the pocket of some unscrupulous rental agent last seen driving a new car? Mister Will and I were witnesses to this as it unfolded. The rule in Mexico is: Always, always deal with the owner. Always.

This all can be a little risky, but to be honest, renting a place was all Mister Will and I had in mind back then. Even in hindsight, renting does have an appeal. No more worries about owners who are delinquent on their dues or a pool pump that's on the fritz. But for those like us fascinated by Mexico, even mesmerized as if seeing a dreamy land of *tequila* and *limones* and wanting to have a stake in it...well, once that enchantment takes over and an opportunity of owning property is in your face, you seize it. That's right, seize it—that's how it can go when rational thoughts get tamped down. No time to wonder if another opportunity will be at your doorstep. This is an opportunity just for you, it seems, and there it is, for you to grab.

So you take the giant step into a Mexican property transfer. After you get past the unsettling terms of ownership and have worked your way through the real estate channels, talked with US and Mexican lawyers and understand the complicated process and the fine print...after all that, you find yourself the proud owner of a Mexican trust and your piece of the Pacific. This you are very happy about. *Salud!* as they say for our "Cheers!"" The Mexican trust is the method that in fact permits a foreigner to own beach property...that is to say, the *building* on the beach property.

After the trust is initiated with a Mexican bank, which is the actual owner and in effect your partner, all that is required is an annual payment, a handsome one all totaled. Ours is somewhere around $550, and that's yearly for the next fifty years. Yes, fifty years. As soon as Mister Will and I got over the shock of such a lifelong arrangement—well, in our case, longer than lifetime—and accepted this Mexican hook for controlling its prime tourist beach areas, and after circumventing the tangled path of actually securing the trust, those yearly bank payments seemed far less daunting. More like a right of passage was our frame of mind. After the fifty years, the trust rolls over to another term, assuming the owner or descendants renew it. The banks make out like bandits on this deal, but what else is a foreigner who is enchanted with Mexican beach property to do?

Our Texan friend George, when his trust was nearing its termination date, was himself nearing, well, his own termination at age ninety-three. Rather than losing his property, which he had owned since the fifties, and rather than starting a new trust when his children didn't show any interest and didn't need any complications down the road, he signed his property over to a longtime Mexican friend. Under that agreement, George was able to live out his life at his home in the comfortable Mexican lifestyle he loved. The comfortable Mexican lifestyle for him meant he could avoid the cursed nursing home scenario back in Texas. Instead, he could get by in his own home with the care of a live-in young Mexican mother with her two school-age daughters. A win-win for all three generations. After he passed, his longtime good friend, a Mexican, took ownership.

Current talk is that Mexico is reconsidering ownership rights in this so-called "restricted zone." The limits date back to 1917 when Mexico worried about US expansionary ambitions, as with Texas, and still in fact the worry continues, as in Mexico's shorelines. Think Cancún, Puerto Vallarta, The Gold Coast. In the 1970s, the exception was created that allowed foreigners to own property through the special trust in partnership with a bank. Now, with its sluggish economy, Mexico sees an opportunity to boost its vacation-home market by allowing foreigners outright ownership, which some argue is long overdue. But until then, the land trusts, *fideicomisos,* are the rule of beach property for foreigners. As mentioned, we foreigners are darn proud to have secured our fifty-year trust.

Keeping Up Upkeep

Stepping into Casa 4 as the new owners didn't happen for six long months after the deal was closed and the 50-year trust initiated; after all, we were in Minnesota for most of the year with Mister Will still heading up his architectural firm. And with property some 2,300 miles away, one doesn't visit often, at least, not on our budget. Hence the delay. So, by the time we did arrive at Posada del Sol that January 2005, car loaded to the roof and expectations even higher, weary yet wired from the four-day roadtrip...we had concocted in our naive little minds a blissful first getaway at our very own casa on the Pacific. The six-month wait had only sweetened our memories of the outdated little place. Possibly a romantic dinner on the beach that first night? Work awaited us, we knew, but we were indomitable with soaring anticipation.

Well-thought out during those months back in Minnesota and during that long, long road trip, our to-do list for a quick makeover of Casa 4 seemed reasonable. Bear in mind, this makeover was just to get by our first season and to feel reasonably comfortable in our new surroundings. Neither of us felt particularly concerned about the work involved and in fact even looked forward to the challenges. "This will be fun!"

In our no-frills way of looking at this new investment into living, Mister Will and I only needed to get rid of the really ugly stuff and then just make do with the rest. Accomplishing that, we would be free to live it up in our new Mexican surroundings. Here's what that actual to-do list looked like: (1) bathtub lodged in shower space...unlodge it, and get rid of first thing! (2) wall-size mural featuring underwater life in the living area...paint-over, (3) floor-to-ceiling wall painting of tropical plant, with actual limbs attached and paper-Mache parrot perched...paint over, ditch the branch, save the parrot, (4) mirrored wall cabinet a.k.a. medicine chest in the kitchen...ditch mirror, save the shelves, (5) odds and ends of plastic light fixtures...ditch and replace, (6) granny-style lacy curtains...ditch, (7) excessive decorative items...ditch, (8) wall relief of angel at the head of the bed...seek help to remove. Note: This massive, plastered angel painted white—garish with overly large lips, bouffant hair, and overly small hands in prayer—ironically projected a sinister presence and would remain with us for many years to come. Difficult to remove with its rebar construction, the heavenly host eventually lost our attention to other more worldly, manageable, and worthwhile matters. We eventually accepted the angel over our bed as funky decor.

All of these to-dos were foremost on our minds when we arrived that day in January 2005, as we gingerly turned the key to our Casa 4 for the first time as the new owners. Click...the heavy, clunky door swung open with a squeak, as if a warning. And in that moment, with both of us now poking our heads inside to see, we knew without a doubt that all of our planned to-dos were put on indefinite hold. "Oh..." we whimpered in unison. We stepped cautiously inside. A thick layer of grimy dirt had settled everywhere. I can't emphasize enough the level...yes, measured accumulation...of dirt. And as if to add more drama, dead cockroaches were poking up through the dirt with a menacing stare. For me, raised by an overly tidy mother whose hands always smelled of bleach, the level of disgust left me lightheaded.

The nine months of sitting idle had transformed Casa 4 into a place abandoned, a place of neglect. The now-dingy sheets covering the furniture added to the dreary scene. What comes to mind is an old western movie with the deserted house left to the elements. Thanks to those loose jalousie windows I mentioned, without a good seal...remember, the romantic ones...thanks to those, the dust and particulate had stealthily found its way inside over those months, like a dirty trick on us while away. How could we not have predicted? Why didn't we arrive with a trunk load of cleaning supplies?

We stopped in our tracks, literally. "No, not going any farther in," we agreed. Our footprints boldly followed us as we retreated to the door again to assess the work ahead. Looking at each other, we sighed, sullen with eyes heavy and mine filling with tears. We sat down on our luggage and took deep breaths as we began our revised plan of attack. Yes, we could do this, but our priorities had changed. Now item 1 on our list was: clean until we drop.

Basic as it is, even housekeeping can become a cultural lesson. No matter our particular owner-type challenges over the years, the one trick Mister Will and I did learn early on to alleviate the enormous task of setup upon arrival was simply to hire it done. Nothing novel about hiring a maid, you say, especially when the cost is minimal. But first consider our particular learned behavior on the matter of housekeeping: We didn't know any better than our tough German upbringing, so as a routine matter, we struggled through the clean up ourselves. Roll up your sleeves and get down to business, that was the drive as accustomed from generations. In those first couple of years, our cleaning efforts to set up Casa 4 upon arrival were at best horribly exhausting and not the lovey-dovey setup we had in mind for our first day at our Mexican getaway. Let's just say that ugly words were spoken. Ah, not paradise as expected. That's enough to hire it done.

In Mexico, domestic housekeeping services are common for us visiting foreigners, providing good for both parties: an extra hand with the housework and extra pesos for someone who needs the work. That said, now many years into this, I still struggle with the idea that another person is in our space, seeing the dirt, and, let's face it, judging. I am fairly sure my meticulous mother is the cause of this. But no matter, I now see the wisdom in hiring it done, most certainly for the initial set up when Mister Will and I arrive from Minnesota, exhausted and foggy. Nothing says welcome to a weary traveler more than an orderly, mostly clean vacation home.

Another reason this concept of hired housekeeping was slow for us to grasp might have been simply the language. Any how-to in a foreign country boils down to adequate command of the language and a general directory of the services available. How can we arrange for a cleaning person without a name and telephone number? Implementation of whatever task that at home would be easy and obvious, like say, google "housekeeping services," just isn't easy or obvious in Mexico. Not even Yellow Pages.

To make my point on this communication hurdle, I'll give you an example of our particular struggle when calling ahead to arrange for casa cleaning prior to our arrival. First, several days before we are due at Casa 4, still at our Minnesota home, we dial up Roque. Simple enough. But wait, dialing up Roque does entail some skill and finesse in these ways: 1) use of the correct international and Mexican telephone codes to make the connection on a landline phone or on a cell phone and 2) use of basic Spanish to get the message across. In our case, we have yet to talk directly with Roque via his cell phone. Why we can't connect remains yet another cell phone mystery for us...something about when and where to add the country code along with the cell designation. With his landline with which we are accomplished at dialing, it is Roque's wife who is home to take the message. She happens to understand no English. Zero. The Spanish words I do manage convey the bare bones, but always super cheery. Here they are translated: "Hello, how are you? [always standard to begin a conversation, then after a similar question back...] Very fine... This is Bergers from Posada del Sol... Please say to Roque... Casa 4 clean...we arrive Monday, January 4... Floors, windows, bathrooms...understand? ...Thank you... Goodbye."

The hobbled message does get across. We arrive, and Casa 4 is suitable for habitation, which is something like a miracle to me. Didn't I need to be there to oversee? Remember, this is nine months of Casa 4 sitting idle. The cover sheets have been removed and folded, patio furniture is back in place outdoors, other furniture has been moved to our normal arrangement (approximately), ceiling fans have been swept of dust, floors and bathrooms have been cleaned, screens have been hosed. And maybe a bit more. Our most recent housekeeper, Maria, likes to show an extra touch by folding the toilet paper as a flower.

The remainder of household tasks will wait for another day: the cupboards and dishes, the reorganizing, and the all-important electronic hookups. But basically, Casa 4 is habitable, a broad-brush once-over after so many months away. Mister Will and I can comfortably settle in on the day of our arrival. My instinct to thoroughly scrub down all hard surfaces can be put on hold. That's the trade-off, I tell my inspector-self for an easy segue into our Mexican life. Just repeating the ever-common *"Mañana"* to myself is oh so useful. *"Mañana."* Breathe easy.

But just once, for the sake of normal communications, I would love to have an in-depth conversation with housekeeper Maria giving a rundown on Casa 4. You know, a casual back and forth. "So, did that hurricane in November bring in a lot more dust?" "Was the dirt deep enough to leave footprints?" "How many dead cockroaches did you find?" "Did you wash the coversheets or just fold them?" "And, just curious, why is the bathroom faucet upside down?" These are details I will never know with my current Spanish.

So this is how we switched to hired help for our setup, really out of necessity. After our nine months away, for a very nominal cost of 300 pesos, which is something like $20, we can comfortably walk into our casa after our overly long road trip, set our luggage down, and feel free to leisurely catch up with our neighbors over cold beers. For that, Maria deserves a very fine payment over and above. For this first day back at Casa 4, at least we can avoid the sight of those ghastly dead cockroaches peeking through the dust. Mister Will and I have crossed another cultural bridge.

If not for the easy flow of life in Mexico, those long hours of grungy cleanup that January afternoon in 2004 just to settle into our Casa 4...just to get to our bed...might have pushed our limits to rash behavior, if not just surly. Despite being exhausted from our four-day road travel and overcome with the new hot, sticky climate, the mess, the foreignness of it all, we sloughed on in tackling the work ahead, holding to just the divined premise from months ago that owning Casa 4 was meant to be. Kindnesses from our North American neighbors that late afternoon serving up quenching watermelon and cold beer brought our personal thermostats down to a comfortable "zoned-out." There from the patio of Casa 4, as we took time to refresh, Mexican tunes were wafting from an establishment across the alley, and our focus lilted to the sounds of the mighty Pacific, the reason for being there. We had arrived, and we would make it.

Handyperson How-To

That reminder to focus, focus, focus on our Mexican prize, this humble Casa 4, energized us for the tasks ahead. Each item on that initial work list offered up new insight into the workings of our new home and our new Mexican community. Each was a colorful challenge beyond our weekend handyman jobs back home, as if we were players in a cross-cultural game for homeowners, rather, *casa* owners as we now proudly called ourselves. "How do we get rid of this bathtub?" and "Where can we find some decent curtains the correct size?" and "What do we do about all these pock marks in the sink?" and "Why are lamps so difficult to find?" Just to name a few at the top of the list, these were our marching orders.

    Paint was the big item for us at Casa 4—as in paint over those murals post haste! And paint, we were soon to learn, especially white paint, seems to be an everlasting need for casa owners on the coast in the harsh elements of ocean, sun, and wind. Paint stores abound with five-gallon buckets of basic white paint. Have you ever taken note of the crisp white hotels lining beach areas? Do you ever wonder how those hotels stay so crisp and bright? That's a lot of white paint, all needing touch up every year from the wear and tear of ocean climate. But, in our case of interior paint, it wasn't white that we were looking for. We wanted bold. This, our first project, was a makeover for those god-awful murals I described, and for those walls, we wanted accents of special hues—you know, Mexican style. Mister Will and I had our shopping challenge.

    Even for such a basic commodity as everyday wall paint, the sales transactions in Mexico, we were quickly to learn, always insist upon an everlasting supply of patience, which, by the way, is more than paid back by a hint of entertainment. One particular shop owner aiming to please dashed out the door and drove down the street for the exact color, leaving Mister Will in charge of his one-man shop. That's when Mister Will, by necessity, learned the Spanish word for owner: *propietario*. What could Mister Will do but stay put and hope that any other transactions could wait. This trusting behavior of the *propietario* is so far removed from our customer-beware skepticism here in the north with any exchange of money for goods that it shakes one's senses. "Are you crazy?" you want to say, "You really will trust me to stay here at your shop while you're gone?" Of course, we don't say it. We go along with a big smile, grateful for a new view of humanity. So we get our paint, our electrical and plumbing parts, our household supplies, all slightly out-of-norm from our familiar products at home and all with cultural lessons and that bit of entertainment as rewards.

The World of Screws...really, that's the translation, *El Mundo de Tornillos,* is probably our best and most entertaining find so far. Tucked into an obscure row of small shops, all with the custom garage-door design almost as if to camouflage, one needs very specific directions with a sense of mission to find it. Our first attempt happened at just that time of the day, early afternoon, when the shop owner was having lunch and resting—at *siesta*—so the door actually was rolled down. Closed, *cerrado.* But when we returned at a later hour, the door was rolled up and the flourishing screw business was in full swing again. Behind the front counter spanning the width of the little establishment were deep aisles of screws to fit any need.

Condo maintenance projects in our Manzanillo can always be a challenge without the likes of an Ace Hardware in the neighborhood, or if one exists, being able to find it tucked in with the little shops. Now in the 21st century, with Mexico's growing economy and upswing into modern conveniences, Manzanillo boasts its very own Home Depot, but that wasn't the case when we were in need of stainless steel screws. Thus, our search for *El Mundo de Tornillos.*

Rust is always the big issue at a coastal city. Rust, the culprit, is a topic as customary and mundane as the weather back home in the north. Folks who decide that the ocean is the ultimate in real estate should be warned: eventually you will pay the price of corrosion damage control. That salt sea air which can soothe the senses enough even to heal a body also chews at metal with a vengeance. Metal anything, be warned! Appliances, sink basins, faucets, electrical contacts, i.e., televisions, the slightest metal in say, a piece of furniture as in a screw...all are doomed by rust. According to Jonathan Waldman who wrote the book *Rust, The Longest War,* rust is the most common natural disaster world wide. That's right, a natural disaster. To get a handle on this statement, consider the damage to bridges, roads, and cars in and around the world's coastal cities. For us on a more personal level, living with sea breezes in open-air homes comes down to replacing a television every two years, accepting pocked kitchen sinks, and getting along with rusted fans, patio furniture, or any ferrous metal that is too darned difficult to replace in our short stay each year. We strive for plastic or stainless steel whatever, whenever possible. Vacation living offers some slack, we like to point out.

It was stainless steel screws that we were after at the now infamous *Mundo de Tornillos*: screws for a couch modification. Screws to withstand the rust. If not for our, shall I say, frugal approach to our newfound winter life at this second home, we could just as well have bought a new couch and ditched the old. But finding a comfortable couch, correct size for our tiny space, color, so forth, would have been a colossal and likely fruitless effort with few stores within reach. At least, we could have tried that route. Remember that here we were on foreign territory, and to seek anything without a good command of the language is a monumental effort. *Gigantesco.*

So the really old wooden Mexican-style couch that came with the place was going to stay. It would have to do. Anyone familiar with old Mexico furniture knows that comfort isn't in the design. A straight back, honestly a 90-degree angle, fits no body that I know. Sit at attention and be miserable; that must have been the idea. And, strange as it is, this straight-back design still is popular across Mexico. Any arrangement of cushions doesn't help with this rigid angle, so our last-ditch effort was to slant the back...literally cut the back off, then fashion it together again with a wing of sorts...odd, I know, but this is what Mister Will, who hobbies in wood projects, dreamed up. So, screws were required to hold the heavy back piece...screws that would not rust. We're back to that.

We set out that day for a quick trip to the closest hardware store to find these special screws, of course no big deal for this sort of purchase back home—just a short drive to the corner Ace Hardware equivalent and problem solved. But three frustrating, sweaty hours later after navigating heavy traffic and new shopping areas, we still were empty-handed. One after another, the helpful clerks at these hardware stores, *ferreteria*, shook their heads no, not here. "*No, señor, no aqui...*". But each did point up or down the road to yet another shop where we might find advice for our new word, "*oxidado.*" Rust. "*No, señor, no aqui*" was the reply at each store.

"Well then, maybe we just need to ask at Martha's, what do you think?" we both suddenly concluded. Of course! Why hadn't we thought of it before. Martha's is the go-to hangout for Manzanillo *gringos*. Just a tiny store on the corner for snacks and drinks, Martha's offers up something possibly more helpful...the sidewalk outside for gathering. Just grab a plastic chair from the stack and park yourself in the circle of gringos under a spindly lime tree. Let the conversation begin...a welcome English conversation, that is. The latest news on fishing, tourist accommodations, shopping, restaurants...that's the usual banter. And Martha herself is helpful with her fluent English. We are not regulars there, but this day we needed help. So it was Martha who steered us to *El Mundo de Tornillos*. Then, armed with the stainless steel screws, Mister Will constructed the ultimate fix to our old Mexican couch. Add new back cushions and *caramba!* We could relax in the comfort of our new/old couch.

Coming in a close second to rust on the misery scale for property owners is the relentless termite. Termites, like rust, are a given in our coastal Mexican climate. I assumed that Mexico had a special curse of the wood-eating insect until I learned that in fact termites can be found in all of our US states except one, Alaska. My logic tells me that since Minnesota is almost as far north as Alaska, I can feel confident that the subject of termite control will not come up when Mister Will and I are in our home state. But alas, not so in our Mexican getaway. Off and on through the years at Posada—whenever the condo budget permits—an exterminator does a sweep of the complex for all crawling and flying insects. This would seem to be a wise investment, although the outcome is never one hundred percent satisfactory. Again, Mexico's standards for contractors don't necessarily meet our standards back home, by a long shot. I plead to you, Mexican Lords of Consumer Safety, where are the warnings, the liability clauses, the masks we see in the US? When the exterminator showed up last year to treat the entire complex, Mister Will and I opted to skip any spraying inside our casa, fearing unknown origin and quantities of toxic, harmful chemicals—this precaution only because of my years in the legal field. "Don't assume anything," as a lawyer once advised. As for the outcome, ants did show up again, but at least no termites. Word is still out on the toxic chemicals more prevalent in developing countries.

Our personal termite story is quite a heart-breaker. Anyone who owns property in Mexico and wishes to buy a piece of, say, wooden furniture, or wooden anything for goodness sakes, knows well enough to stay away from pine, fir, plywood, any of those soft woods...at least if not treated. When Mister Will, a woodworker of the utmost caliber, masterfully created a lovely coffee table for our Casa 4, with inlaid stone tiles and a glass top for displaying our favorite seashells, then hauled it in our car all those 2,300 miles to Manzanillo, he knew to use cedar for the legs. Cedar doesn't sit well with termites. But the wood he selected for the framework of those stone tiles was plywood, a veritable delicacy for termites. Situated as it was above the floor with the cedar legs in between, the plywood, one would assume, would be out of range for any termite action.

Not so. That next season when we arrived and entered the gate of Posada del Sol, my attention immediately was drawn to an unusual sight on our patio, where I saw my favorite piece of furniture, the lovely handcrafted coffee table, out of place now sitting outside. "What?" I gasped as I hurried to our patio. "Why on earth has Roque moved our coffee table outside to the patio subject to the elements?" I was frantic. But up close, we understood. We could see in devastating detail the work of termites while we had been gone those nine months. Beyond repair, the coffee table now sat with chews and conga lines etched into the craftsmanship, with the invading termites still at work. Roque had simply moved the table out of the casa before our arrival. Mister Will, accepting the fate of his work and defeat to the termites, threw his artistic piece into the dumpster, inlaid stone tiles and all. "Well, that's that!" he said, swiping his hands clean of the matter and continuing on with the unpacking as if the disaster were just a broken plate. I trudged along with the work, muttering something about "this god-forsaken place." Not only had we lost the nicely appointed furniture piece, but we were back to square one without a functional coffee table, and shopping for one seemed like an extra aggravation when all we wanted to do was get organized and kick back. Comic relief, however, can be handy. Roque, being Roque, offered a simple explanation to reinforce the lesson: Lacking sufficient English words, instead he gestured stuffing food in his mouth, and with a wide grin he said,

"Comida para los termitas!" Translation: Lunch for the termites.

The projects have been many and varied, and each with a "human interest story," as the media calls it when reporting on encounters with heart. Enrique, the upholsterer, who has expertly and for a nominal fee refashioned literally all of our cushioned furniture over the years; Mago's two sons, the computer geeks who expertly and for a nominal fee reconfigured our ailing computer and returned to do it again and again for no fee; the nameless Spanish-only handyman-plumber from down the street who expertly and for a nominal fee solved our washing machine malfunction...these are but a few of the stories that bond our hearts with our fellow Mexicanos.

Human interest aside, the simple fact is that every last detail of this aforementioned hard work and sweat over the years—the frustrations, the costs, the worries, the back-breaking labor—could have been totally, completely, without a doubt avoided had we chosen the more popular option: renting. This is why owning property can have such a bad rap...it's labor intensive and...not to overlook even small hardware items, as in stainless steel screws...costly. Consequently, I advise: Know how much you like your stuff. Really, how important is it for you to own your environment?

The people we know who rent, and there are a lot of them, do so for these reasons I've set out. Those who rent are free to spend their time, well, vacationing. With no responsibilities for how the place is maintained, they simply notify so-and-so manager if, say, the air conditioner quits or a scorpion shows up in their bathroom.

We, on the other hand, look at our time away in a different light, not so much as a "vacation," but more like carrying on our usual activities in a different climate and culture. For us, that change of climate and culture is revitalizing in itself. All of our tasks are approached in a slightly different framework, and sometimes the task becomes a challenging puzzle of "how to get this done with what's available." In the case of the coffee table, we switched out a table from the patio and the result suited us just fine. No shopping. Mister Will does his best to fix or replace whatever is failing and consults regularly with our neighbor across the pool, who also is handy, to exchange ideas and borrow tools. And vice versa. For backup, Mister Will consults trusty Roque who, if he cannot resolve the problem himself, keeps at reach a current list of workers in the various trades, i.e., electrical, plumbing, all-around fixit. The good news is that in Mexico, labor is cheap. So that's a positive for us in this ownership dilemma. And let's not forget the colorful cultural exchanges.

I suspect a majority of foreigners owning Mexican property even find satisfaction in home maintenance. They are good at it and even look at maintenance as a hobby—you know, skilled at plumbing, electrical, carpentry, painting, general fix-its. Like the satisfaction of nesting. You know who you are. Just as back home, these certain special folks are good at home repairs and even look forward to a challenging project. "See honey, I fixed it!" This I see in Mister Will. He and a couple of our North American neighbors swap tools and know-how like the guys from "This Old House." To top off that fulfillment, they get the privilege of a cultural immersion of sorts tending to all the basics of everyday living in Mexico, even if the discussion at the local *ferreteria* is about a leaky toilet.

When guests arrive, however, that's a different dynamic all together—that's when we who own our habitations switch to vacation mode. That's when we bring out the snorkel gear, the boogie board, and every brochure we've ever collected on

Manzanillo sights. That's when we put aside any household projects and get in vacation mode ourselves.

These then are some considerations for anyone with the notion of owning Mexican beach property, you people who really like your own stuff. Sound not so bad? Doable? Read on.

Chapter 8 – Owning, Part II
Lesson: Know Your Condo Etiquette in Spanish

After getting through the intricacies and legalities of owning Mexican beach property and accepting the reality of environmental risks to your property, i.e., rust, termites, and let's not overlook earthquakes and hurricanes, still an owner faces the complications of simple shared living in a foreign culture. Welcome to condo-world *Mexicano*. Accepting the weighty fifty-year trust along with serious wear and tear on your beach investment is small potatoes compared to condo association dynamics, cross-culture-wise. But maybe that's just me, preferring that personal affairs are kept to oneself.

Coming from our own sweet, privately owned Minnesota home where all decisions are ours alone, Mister Will and I find the concept of sharing common space, and the costs associated, to be restrictive...and every so often, annoying. That, of course, we know is the trade-off for easy, carefree maintenance and secure (mostly) accommodations in a far away place. But, so we are learning, whether abroad or at home, communal living is where many of our peers in this retirement life are headed. Having no prior experience with condo associations, we can't speak to the workings of those back in the US, but we do know for absolute certain that in Mexico, condo owners from the north best ride loose in the saddle. The next best piece of advice: learn Spanish.

Naturally, this communal living setup obligates owners to pay a yearly fee for common area maintenance, a large part of which for us is Roque's salary for keeping the place in tip-top condition. Did I mention we all love him? Then, aside from his salary, the fees basically cover upkeep of the pool and community spaces, fresh paint yearly for condo exteriors, the gas utility, and any miscellaneous maintenance expenses for the common property. That's the financial part. We owners also agree to abide by the rules of the association (yet to be fully understood) and to attend the annual meeting, either in person or by proxy. It's this cross-cultural annual meeting that I want to make a point of here.

A condo annual meeting here at home might just be a boring duty, but in Mexico, *la junta,* definitely is not boring. Descriptions come to mind: challenging (as in two languages back and forth and sometimes at the same time), arduous (as in double the time to allow for any translations), perplexing (as in no protocol or strict protocol within the same meeting), unsettling (as in no resolution to nagging agenda items). It challenges not only our cross-cultural neighborliness and sense of good business acumen, but it challenges our grip of language, which of course is the undergirding for any informed conversation with our Mexican co-owners. Not boring. Even for the hardiest, a more apt descriptive name among us gringo owners soon became "the dreaded annual meeting."

As if a meeting of minds over shared ownership isn't enough of a challenge, just try it in two languages. Any agenda items bordering on the negative seemingly get ramped up to a feverish pitch in a mix of Spanish and English. One word misspoken, misunderstood, or just plain missed can turn a discussion from good to really bad. Blood pressures rise. The Mexican women start smoking.

We from *el norte* at Posada are in the minority with our Mexican neighbors—four to six—so it's natural that at least two-thirds of the conversations are in Spanish. Then think for example how a majority will sometimes take over the conversation in any group; well that makes those odds for English in this group even worse. Who of us gringos can even muster the courage to get an English word in edgewise? Or a Spanish word, if we happened to know it. That said, however, we from the north have no ground to complain; after all, we are the foreigners in this embracing culture. In the early years at Posada we relied on Spanish translations by one or two of the Mexican owners. That's handy, we thought at first, but we soon realized that these Mexicans were just stepping in to help out and didn't necessarily have a full grasp of English, just as if, for instance, I tried to translate our English for the Mexicans. In addition, we English folks needed to keep in mind that the translations could be slanted, not intentionally, for the Mexicans' personal motivations, which needed to be factored into the equation. So the interpretations were always suspect. Sometimes a fifteen-minute oration by one of the Mexicans on a particular issue, as the pros and cons of switching to individual water meters for our units, is translated into one sentence such as this: "Roque will check with the city about the overdue water bill." Hold it...who exactly is paying for what?

Not until recent years did we have the good sense to hire a bona fide translator, a Canadian-born Mexican resident, as it worked out. Still, even with a translator, discussions tend to shoot off into the unknown, the main fault I see being that of whoever is presiding, to keep items on track. "Back to the issue, please," I raise my hand to beg an explanation. Quite possibly the translator should lead the meeting alongside the president. One group at the end of the table will be discussing the state of our budget, while another, the new lock for the front gate, both discussions in Spanish. We from *el norte* mostly just get the drift.

My personal goal repeatedly has been, once and for all, for the sake of decency in this cross-cultural experience as a property owner, study the dammed Spanish! Get a handle on conjugating those tricky verbs that are critical. Action words...we need them, and we need them in a proper tense. Critical real-life example: "He paid his fee" or "He will pay his fee." Just the proper forms of "to be" would solve many a mistaken communication. But sadly, as of this date, my goal has fallen short, and I remain in the present tense. Perhaps my latest go at it might be this handy language app I hear about in the news, apparently so helpful at my fingertips. Just get the app.

So, then, the dreaded annual meeting remains a dreaded obligation. We from *el norte* bob our heads between the speakers trying to pick up a familiar word or two, most likely the nouns, at the same time appearing as though we clearly understand. Why not at least signal our confusion? Instead, we nod a perplexed "Um, huh." No real headway there because the Mexicans continue in their Spanish. Finally, exasperated, one of us holds up a flimsy hand to ask for a translation. *"Ingles, por favor?"*

Well, you can easily understand why this style of meeting, with the back and forth translations, the interruptions, and sidebars by both groups, can easily last twice as long as a normal meeting. We leave the meeting exhausted and ready for a stiff drink. Not only that, we leave confounded, wondering, "So, what just happened here?" Roberts Rule of Law just never caught on in Mexico.

And that's on a good day. Contentious issues have driven certain owners to abruptly get up and huff away or to move their chairs as in picking sides. Sound like elementary school? There have been the threatened lawsuits over who owes what, the subtle finger-pointing about personal allocations, the manipulations for unapproved additions to condos, the accusations over improper accounting, and the overly angry voices venting on when or when *not* to cut down the coconuts.

The cutting of coconuts, by the way, is a highly sensitive issue that we gringos have learned not to take lightly, and in that light, the issue deserves to be mentioned here. The fact that Mister Will's hammock is strung between two palm trees that produce coconuts the size and weight of bowling balls doesn't necessarily worry our Mexican owners. Beware of your own doing, that's the Mexican approach. Unlike the US, Mexico isn't entangled with laws of liability, and I personally see that as a plus. For our Mexican neighbors, it's the ripening of the coconuts that's important, not the safety of some clueless foreigner lounging under a coconut ready to drop. Too bad if it does, *senor*. I for one will sidestep, zig-zag, serpentine, walk around my usual path in and out of Posada, whatever it takes to avoid walking directly under a clump of ripe coconuts. Even a baby one has potential for knock-out. And they do fall. Hearing that familiar thud, we *gringos* say a collective "Ah hah!" as a sort of confirmation that, yes, this is our evidence as we spot it on the ground.

"See there," we point Roque to the fallen *coco* there on the lawn or the walkway. Roque tosses the coconut aside and with a broad smile says, "*Si peligroso."* Translation: Yes, dangerous.

The timing for these ripe coconuts is critical as well, all to coincide with the biggest holiday in Mexico, *Semana Santa*, or as we know, Easter week. Fresh coconut milk apparently is the drink of gods and, as we recently learned, it aids in belly disorders. We from *el norte* watch as our Mexican neighbors hurry with their pitchers to collect all they can when Roque machetes the coconuts. We also have observed Roque reporting swiftly to the beach with his machete when summoned by our Mexican neighbors ordering up fresh *coco* drinks in the shade of their umbrellas. After literally years of back and forth as to when exactly the palm trees might be trimmed and the coconuts cut, our Posada del Sol has finally settled into a compromise of sorts, although we from *el norte* finally get it that we remain at the whims of the Mexican owners. The compromise goes like this: The palm trees towering over walkways—and Mister Will's hammock (which happens to occupy a common area, oops)—are mostly trimmed, meaning the larger ones are cut but the smaller coconuts are left hanging to mature into a bounty of coconuts sometime later, likely after we *gringos* have gone north and just in time for their Easter festivities. The *Mexicanos* are wise to our preferred vacation schedule now, which is to avoid the Easter crowds, a win for both sides of the *coco* issue. We pack to go home just as those crowds of *Mexicanos* arrive.

Whether it's the revered coconuts or delinquent owners that is the topic at our meetings, the contentious issues are like red hot jalapeños in our very own *novela*. We U.S. and Canadian citizens struggle mightily with this feisty behavior, but to our great amazement, our Mexican neighbors typically end a meeting, no matter the rancor, with formal handshakes, smiles, and bids of farewell for the day. Musicians could just as well be launching into a soothing ballad to end the dramatic interplay. Mexico's social etiquette trumps rudeness every time, no matter the discussion. We from *el norte* remain puzzled. "Hold on just a minute..." we want to say. "What about the arguments, the insinuations, the blame-calling? Where do we stand on those issues?" To our way of thinking, the group should disperse all huffy and disgruntled. And certainly with no handshakes.

Certain condo issues have dogged us for years, with no positive end in sight, as in unpaid condo fees and unpaid federal taxes. The most grievous offense of unpaid condo fees falls to one certain Mexican owner, Smooth Talker. He seems to hold us co-owners hostage with the cockeyed notion that his permanent presence at Posada keeps the place secure which, he argues, offsets his share of the fees. To my understanding, no one ever agreed to this. His yearly fees for common area maintenance are overdue by decades. His fast-talking promises are questionable at best. But who will argue with this man who suggests that he might or might not keep a watchful eye on your *casa* all those months we are away?

Then we have the burden of unpaid federal taxes also mounting exponentially over the years. These taxes involve complicated beach assessments for properties infringing upon what is known as the Federal Zone. Apparently, a certain distance of beach is designated as "Federal Zone"—in other words public property. Questions arise however as to where exactly the measurement begins and ends; changeable it would seem with the ebb and flow of the ocean. Who of us English speakers can communicate fluently regarding this local issue, or even understand it? You see where we gringos fail on resolving this matter. Here again, Smooth Talker, in his continual effort to impress, claims he has certain ins with the federal authorities to argue on behalf of Posada. To date, Posada is still in arrears to the tune of let's say *muchos, muchos pesos*. And Smooth Talker still is in arrears to Posada for his annual fees.

Always a ruckus is brewing. Whether it's the cost of a concrete wall built for privacy from the public access or whether it's the blatant infringement in using the common areas, the Mexican owners stand their ground. We from *el norte* do our best to understand the arguments, but in the end, again, we fail for lack of adequate language skills and basic understanding of cultural norms. Who of us is well enough versed in Spanish to negotiate with contractors for a sizable concrete wall to benefit all Posada owners or even to comprehend the nuances of Mexican social norms when the issue is that of private space? We get a no-passing grade. We throw up our hands in frustration. We must rely on a Mexican for the ongoing operation of our condo association with all the attendant business matters pertaining to our Posada del Sol.

The issue of Posada owners who rent out their units is something of a thorny problem too. Whenever the discussion at home is about our little winter place in Mexico, invariably after the first question, "Aren't you afraid?" is this one: "Do you rent it out?" It turns out that folks are always on the lookout for a good vacation spot to rent. And, it turns out, many folks who own a condo are eager to rent it and make a little cash on the investment, understandably. A win-win, yes? Well, at our Posada, with no enforceable rules on anything, the rental practices by various owners, in this case namely the Mexicans, brings into question what is fair for those who choose not to rent. Think, for example, fairness regarding extra common costs for pool maintenance, water for pool and laundry, general wear and tear on the common grounds. Some condos in the area actually charge a daily occupancy fee, not only for renters but for the owners themselves. Not so at Posada for us owners, but recently we began to charge a daily occupancy fee for renters. Collecting it is yet another step.

The Mexicans who rent their condos ironically are those who are slow in their yearly payments, and they also resist mightily the daily occupancy fee. This is where diplomacy and firm rules meet head on. If this situation were here at home where we share the same language, we would give that offender a good talking to and work out a payment program. As it is, we gringos pay our dues and depend upon our Mexican manager to collect from delinquent owners. She tiptoes the fine line between cultures to wrestle out a payment and still maintain a respectful relationship with all of us. This is in store for us at each dreaded annual meeting…who owes how much and what exactly is the state of our budget. Then we move on to the next topic. Again, even-tempered communication in two languages can be hard work.

While the notion of renting our casa is always a possibility, like a fallback, I hold that at no time in these eighteen years have Mister Will and I seriously considered it. Could we use the money? Of course. Would it be worth the hassle and uncertainty in foreign business dealings far from home? Absolutely not. Certainly many if not most condo owners in Mexico do rent their units by way of a reputable agent; they recover their costs and have a beach home at their disposal and, in the best scenario, on their own terms. Somehow, that isn't us. Some days I wish it were so. Quite possibly our low-profile, low-cost Posada del Sol allowed us to embrace it for ourselves only. And the fact that Mister Will and I happened on our Casa 4 at that moment in our lives when it was possible —recall the notion of providence— well, the humble old *casa* seems reserved for just us. Even a passing thought of strangers in our quarters seems wrong. So we continue to shoulder all of the costs and hassle associated with condo living, but with smug satisfaction. Plus, all of that "stuff" I mentioned in the first section of this chapter...all of that we can leave and know it's there when we come back.

This was all in store for us as owners now at Posada del Sol, a condominium association that, we had yet to learn, had not yet been officially registered with the Mexican government when we bought our casa in 2004. Did we know enough even to ask this? Of course not...I mean, why would we question the workings of Mexican property law? Entranced as we were, we could only get out heads around the idea of getting this deal of a lifetime. Certainly not Mexican property law. Now eighteen years later we only have begun to understand the requirements of a legitimate Mexican condo association. Engaging a full-time professional manager for the association is a wise bet; this we now know.

The Posada organization was, shall I say, a bit loose back then with the original Minnesota-Wisconsin-Iowa owners not thoroughly versed in Mexican real estate. They bought and sold with title transferring at least in the US, but only maybe in Mexico and with no real leverage as to owners who didn't pay. We have learned now that this sort of leverage with those type of losers only happens with a properly registered association. Otherwise, sorry.

In our very first season at Posada we learned of at least two Mexican owners who were in arrears for a year or even several years, those staggering amounts varying, depending on who gave us the information. Sobering state of the account, you might say, for us newbies from *el norte,* having just invested in our dream winter getaway. Coming from our background of tidy accounts and prudent spending, we simply could not comprehend that an owner might be in arrears. What are the consequences? Why can an owner continue living at Posada when past fees are long overdue? This isn't fair! Well, in Mexico at least, a condo association for any legal leverage must have that illusive certificate of registration wrangled from the high court. One condo group without the official registration did actually take action, vigilante style; utilities were cut off to that offending owner. Next best solution: pure hounding of that particular delinquent owner.

In 2007, Posada del Sol did pursue full status as a condominium, but after numerous tries involving a maze of paperwork and *muchos pesos* submitted to the *notario,* the result was just an English translation of the original condo document. It's true, a translation in itself was a victory. But the full-blown process for becoming a legitimate Mexican condo association would remain undone. *Incompleto.* To date, we see no evidence of progress along this front. Hence, no legal remedies for owners in arrears.

Oh, the tests and trials of living our dream of owning Mexican beach property. The key goals for us from the north, of course, are simple: Peace and tranquility in our vacation home for our extended stays. Is this too much to ask? We pay our association fees and expect a magical holiday. This quite possibly is where rentals get a high mark; none of our friends who rent have ever stewed about the cost of, say, repair to the seawall. They are never even bothered with the idea. The owners will do it.

In our Posada, with a majority of Mexican owners, we face an uphill cultural battle just understanding the rational. What seems to us as a blatant disregard for timely payment of one's fair share, to our Mexican counterparts might be a temporary holdup in payment when juggling the funds for another obligation with more priority. Think: a family concern. The Mexican will eventually get around to the payment. But this we North Americans don't know. If we aren't careful with our mindfulness, where's the peace and tranquility? The days that Mister Will and I have thrown up our suntanned arms in defeat...given up on making sense of any particular condo issue whatsoever...those are the days in fact that we sense again a bit of peace and tranquility. As if by design, a soothing Mexican tune from across the alley seems directed just for us. We jump in the pool for a swim. Let it go. "*No problemo,*" as they say, Mexican style.

After years of hyperventilating on these issues, Mister Will and I are either dulled from the tiresome story of who hasn't paid or we are resigned with Mexico as it is. Either way, we shrug it off and enjoy our own space of Casa 4 at Posada del Sol amid whatever hostilities may be brewing at the time. We are comfortable in the fact that we are not those offenders; we are timely in paying our yearly dues, and sometimes even early.

At some point in all these years of Mexican condo living, Mister Will and I learned that basic human trust and intuitive instincts are best put into play when concerns arise with our Latino neighbors and their culture. Best to ensure a good night's sleep, which honestly is what we all are after. We reflect on what our good Mexican friend told us long ago: Mexicans owning a second home on the coast certainly have the wherewithal to come up with annual condo payments, and they most certainly will not allow the property to fall into disrepair. So, we trust the system insofar as upkeep – as to those owners staying current with payments, however, perhaps a common vote could invoke incentives or consequences. One such consequence might be at least to threaten that gas will be turned off if payment is not made by a certain date.

I would be remiss if I didn't nag on the importance of thorough research ahead of time. Our experience illustrates that before signing on the dotted line for a dream Mexican beach property, the basic elements of condo living and soundness of management should be addressed. Naturally intertwined with this sort of information is that illusive colorful Mexican flair, the dynamics of which can make or break a pleasant living situation. Be diligent in your homework so you have no surprises.

Except for the fact that our Posada is likely one of the oldest condominiums in the area and naturally has more history, my story just laid out is not in the least bit unusual. Comparing notes with foreign owners like ourselves at other condo organizations, Mister Will and I come away bonded with them in the recurring themes of delinquent Mexican owners and problematic accounting. "No kidding?" we say. "So how do you enforce penalties for late payments?" and the discussion goes on over our happy hour. We feel like family as we commiserate, but the issues will persist until we agree on consequences.

Mister Will and I didn't do the homework when we bought, that's clear. I blame it on that basic trust principle we both learned growing up in the Midwest. We didn't know and couldn't have imagined the questionable circumstances of old Posada del Sol built in the sixties there on the coastal road of Manzanillo with so many old grievances under the radar. Consider a Mexico for hardy and fearless vacationers sixty years ago, not modernized Mexico we know today. Consider too the many ways we foreigners can go wrong when we are not versed in another culture's business practices.

In our defense, those many years ago when we were considering the purchase, Mister Will and I did go so far as to ask questions about foreign acquisitions. But this was back home where we had English-speaking professionals from whom to seek advice. That term "foreign acquisitions" straight away has the vibe of a warning, right? Foreign acquisitions for many of us brings to mind shady investments, money laundering, offshore accounts, and who knows? Some of the online stories were downright scary, describing properties scooped up by the Mexican government in the case of improper or incomplete documents. Mexico, we have learned, is the land of layered Spanish edicts, colonial governances, and bribes. Our lawyer acquaintance in Minnesota researched as best he could and then steered us to a title company. Admittedly, he didn't have access to Mexican law. But title insurance—that he knew. After plunking down several hundred dollars for title insurance, we felt, well, grounded. Interestingly, a Mexican *notario* told us later "*no necesito, no necesito.*" Whom were we to believe? Mexican law or our own code of real-estate-transaction common sense? No matter; Mister Will and I keep a tight, proud hold on our title insurance. At least to a US citizen, title insurance even in Mexico suggests an upstanding property owner. And upstanding property owners we are. The reality nags, however, that US laws carry no weight in Mexico, just as Mexican laws carry no weight in the US.

If this comes off too heavy, hold on for a look at your Mexican community.

Chapter 9 – Owning, Part III
Lesson: Know Your Community Doings

Yes, of course, community is an important factor to consider, not only for buyers but also in the case of renters. We pick and choose our vacation spots, best as we can, based on our living preferences. But the deep-down sense of community that I am talking about here is what a prospective buyer should weigh heavily. In a sense, buying into the community. Mister Will and I did not necessarily do this. Our first attraction was the ocean and the out-of-the-blue opportunity. We jumped on it...and evaluated the community later.

The Setting
Suffice it to say, the character of the community likely is what attracts a prospective owner in the first place and will shape the experience for years to come. Upscale? Busy?

Thriving? Peaceful? This after all is an investment into happy, healthy living. Choose wisely.

Our particular location is on the main boulevard, which not only is busy with traffic and thriving businesses but also attracts big community events. I wonder, had we weighed the pros and cons of sinking our investment into this busy setting, would we have looked elsewhere? Probably not, as hyped up as we were, but a wise buyer should consider all the angles. Our busy boulevard has its pluses and minuses; pluses are the vitality and convenience of shopping/restaurants/public transportation, and minuses are the traffic noise and dirt.

One example of our particular busy location is the annual mardi gras parade staged two nights on our boulevard. Who knew that Mexico celebrates this French tradition, unless of course taking into account the Catholic origins. With its gigantic semi-truck floats, blaring speakers, and scantily clad dancers, the parade is a highlight of the community. Crowds just outside our Posada gate begin gathering early afternoon and wait for the parade, which doesn't begin until after sunset. All this while individuals with boom boxes are blaring local tunes and souvenir vendors are walking the boulevard, which is already cleared of traffic. Mister Will and I hold fast at Posada in fear of losing our parking space. The event envelops us.

For us, the parade might be fun for a few minutes watching at the curb, but the sheer volume of amped-up music with the truck floats honking horns on and on soon grows tiresome and even painful. This is especially so in the late hours when we are back in our casa attempting sleep. Then, oddly, for a second night, the parade repeats, this as a double reward or just in case you missed it, but this time starting from the opposite direction.

Understandably, the subject of a mega parade marching down our very own boulevard two nights in a row in late

February never came up when we were dealing with the seller. Surely, anyone buying property on this busy boulevard, given a minute to think about the pros and cons, can conceive of many and assorted community doings in this prime location; after all, the property is not on a deserted stretch of beach.

Sometimes the ocean itself can be a negative. I know, this sounds far-fetched for those paying high prices for a spot on the ocean. Isn't the ocean a main attraction? Well yes, but not necessarily at your door step. We in fact have friends who have been frightened by the crashing waves so close to their quarters, even to cause the condo buildings to shake. I too can relate to this fear. Over the years I've found that the ocean is soothing to me, yes, but only from a distance. Our friends, who happen to rent, moved from their ocean-side condo with the crashing waves to a condo where the ocean isn't even visible; it's a couple of blocks away. They are surrounded by lovely grounds with a pool, a tranquil setting. The peace and quiet is perfect for them, and they experience the ocean on their terms.

Added Value

As property owners, Mister Will and I do pay our utilities and taxes (both minimal as compared to Minnesota), and we are always on the lookout for new developments and how they might affect our Casa 4, value-wise. Here's an example: Several years ago a really top-notch four-story condo sprouted up next door. More recently, out from the alleyway between our Posada and this upscale condo sprung a classy steak house, and it continued to maintain a good business, well, that is until the owners had a fight. Still, for us, not bad real estate, wouldn't you say, for our little 1960s motel/condo presence in this popular area?

But a heavy-traffic, more upscale location doesn't necessarily mean an added value for the owner. Our open-air living arrangement necessarily means more noise from outside. Our busy street attracts a new bar or taco stand every year, it seems, and that translates to loud music, most often electric, not acoustic, and most often just as we are going to bed. Let's face it, *Mexicanos* are night people who love their music. On one particular night I recall two competing bars across the street blaring old-time Mexican and Frank Sinatra, an outdoor concert down the block blaring Mexican-country, and ramped-up car stereos in the public access lot blaring Mexican hip-hop. We were blasted until sunrise. That's when we suggested ear plugs for our guests. But, interestingly for us to acknowledge, after the years of experience and a certain built-in adjustment for such jarring differences from our quiet northern home, Mister Will and I have learned to sleep on.

Over our eighteen years now, we have seen Manzanillo develop, but tourist growth in particular has been slow as compared to the high-end beach towns, i.e., Cancún, Puerto Vallarta, Mazatlán. If, for example, Puerto Vallarta has ten new high-rise condos in the works, Manzanillo has one...maybe. Still, Manzanillo has developed. Franchises have trickled in after Walmart made its mark some years ago, not always a good thing the way we see it for those local family businesses we love. And most recently a high-end shopping mall landed on our beach. Lordy, we speculate, how will it survive in this everyday working port city?

We in fact love the notion that tourist attraction is not a top priority. We people of Manzanillo are somehow above the allure of glitzy beach marketing and are not like those folks in Cancún, Puerto Vallarta, Mazatlán, and so on. Just ask any of us. Our city doesn't really need the tourists, we like to say. Manzanillo is all about the port, which just happens to be the largest on Mexico's Pacific coast. We brag. Tourists may come and go, but it's the port that is the business of Manzanillo, and any newcomer quickly sees this just with a glance out into the bay; at any given hour, two, three, maybe a half-dozen container ships are awaiting orders for docking.

So the port seems to us an added value. Naturally, watching the ship movements and maneuvers has become something of an entertainment for us out-of-towners. That fascination translates to our overall satisfaction, as in, "Hey, we have the plus of watching port activities right here where we live."

Ship-watching is not rapid-paced entertainment certainly, but it's fascinating in its own right. We wonder what the containers in fact contain...electronics, cars, knock-off plastic shoes, Mexico souvenirs made in China? We wonder about the ship's origin... Any castaways? We wonder how and if these ships are inspected... Drugs? And how in the name of Saint Christopher do all of the unloaded containers travel to their intended places? The port poses like a giant multi-dimensional board game for us observing from afar. And now we have an internet site with a map of our bay in real time giving the name and destination of each ship.

About once a week the entertainment heightens when word spreads that a cruise boat is leaving dock. The departure is always in tune with sunset, as if staged for dramatic effect: the splendor of it all, with a romantic call of sorts from the ship's horn in the distance, a puff of smoke from the stack as evidence of engines running, and then finally, the majestic boat, this seven-story hotel, is inching out to sea, then once past the tug boats, picking up speed. The little lights twinkle from the ship's quarters, and swags of festive colored lights certainly suggest partying on board. We watch with our binoculars from the sea wall, as we imagine the ship's passengers are looking with binoculars back at us on land, until the boat fades into the Pacific and the night. Then we return to our respective *casas* with toothy grins and a sense of pride in this, our tough Manzanillo port city which in fact has luxury cruise boats too.

That slightly snobbish attitude about our real town has to take into account too the reality of a dirty downside, and I do mean dirty: Manzanillo's thermoelectric plant. Do take note of environmental issues of your potential purchase. Even on that first trip in 2004, Mister Will and I wondered about the thick plumes of dark smoke circling up from stacks faintly visible far in the distance of our hotel balcony. I questioned it too when we negotiated for our casa, then again and again and again over the years. This was no minor issue for me, one a bit fanatical about health issues, studying breaking news on everything from bad/good cholesterol to good/bad fat-free foods and the bad/bad ever-growing body mass index. Then to top it off, this new worry: air quality. The answers to my questions, mostly gleaned from online searches, my furrowed brow with nose to the computer screen, ranged between a serious "Going to be fixed soon...the fuel will be clean gas instead of dirty coal...maybe next year, soon anyway..." and a light-hearted "You know how it is in Mexico to get anything done...*mañana!* The thread of hope I clung to was a group of wealthy expats and locals who happened to own the pricest homes in the area. And their pricey homes happened to be in the direct path of that dirty air in the prevailing winds. If *they* were on the issue, then something eventually would be done.

Well, *mañana* finally happened a few years ago and, interestingly, with no real hoop-la. Certainly, I expected everyone to be bonkers—like myself—over this green development after all those years of dirty air. Well, in fact, *El Presidente* did visit, and we must assume that while we were back in Minnesota, the community cheered on this massive project. I'll even wager that *mariachi* bands were involved.

We foreigners who soak up the warm climate at will for brief periods resume our lives in the north with no particular air-quality concerns, or for that matter, any other concern about our Mexican community, until the calendar says it's time to head south again. But I for one will continue my gone-bonkers cheer each year I first set gaze again over the Pacific at the clear skies over our Manzanillo: an overdue breath of fresh air.

Activities to Suit

Another feature of our particular community is in fact a personal preference not associated with beach property and likely not of major importance to a majority of prospective buyers in Mexico. After all, if you're looking for beach property, your main focus is, well, the beach. I mention it here as an example of how priorities vary for each of us, worthwhile considerations in eyeing property to buy and sometimes really, really important. Exactly what is it about a location that says "Yes!"

In fact, a key selling point for our Casa 4 was that old, dusty outdoor running track I mentioned in Chapter 3 located about six blocks down the boulevard, of course, off the beach. For the two of us accustomed our entire adult lives to daily workouts and runs, that neighborhood feature clinched the deal. If in another scenario, we were to find ourselves in a place that offered little or no options for running, we would have to think long and hard about an alternative for exercise. When this outdoor track presented itself in our negotiations with the seller, well, Mister Will checked a bold "Yes!" on our list of must-haves.

Those of you familiar with getting around by foot in Mexico know that outdoor exercise like we know it back home with paths and wide-open spaces is hard to come by, well, except for those all-inclusive deals that mimic fantasy island in a warm climate. The all-inclusive even seem designed to accommodate the workout needs of North Americans. Some tourist areas on the coast might have a lovely pier walk, *malecón,* which is not only great for the exercise but fantastic *vistas.*

In true Mexico, a nice walk entails two words of caution: 1) traffic and 2) foot plant. Sidewalks often are very narrow, say the width for one person, and often with irregularities. One must be in the moment at all times. Even beach walking if in deep sand at an angle can lead to orthopedic visits. Just ask Mister Will about his ordeal with plantar fasciitis. So you see the appeal for us, seeking to find our athletic lifestyle in a southern climate, now learning about this workout facility nearby. Was this an auspicious omen? The track our lynchpin? We could picture our happy workout YMCA selves in this setting.

This outdoor track, Cinco de Mayo, as it is named, is one of the best-kept secrets about our Manzanillo. In fact, among the other North Americans who, like us, spend weeks or months in Manzanillo, it might as well be a secret. Up until recent years, the two of us on most mornings were the only gringos at the track. Now we see at least a sprinkling more. In our travels in Mexico over the years, Mister Will and I have had other occasions to search out good exercise options, whether an indoor gym at a hotel or, if when really searching, an outdoor soccer field circled with a dusty track similar to our *Cinco de Mayo.* These community activity areas do exist. My point is this: When considering a Mexican property, find the setting that suits you. Look for it. Whether it is a nearby golf course, a gym, perhaps tennis courts, the added feature in your very own Mexican beach community can make your property very personal.

In recent years, with the port expansion and pesos pouring in from the Korean developer, someone in that higher echelon had the foresight to overhaul our Cinco de Mayo track. Recall our ill-conceived charity efforts at the facility earlier. With the Korean developer, the dirt track was converted to state-of-the-art Tartan, the bleachers and surrounding buildings were painted, a new fence was installed, the infield/soccer field was resodded, and most impressively...garbage bins were added. Now this facility is absolutely embraced by the community. Whether it's soccer, basketball, volleyball, baseball, boxing, aerobics, swimming, running, or just plain hanging out with the family on a stroll around the track...it's the place to be, morning or night. More and more we see an occasional foreigner or two out for a morning walk or run at the track. We size it up as another one of those community efforts that can only boost our Casa 4 value. But that aside, it beautifully fits our particular health plan. Our outdoor YMCA.

La Securidad

And finally, in sizing up a community with the intention of owning property in Mexico, there is the issue that gets all the media attention back home, sadly: Mexico's drug traffic. Yes, our Manzanillo has drug traffic. Yes, we read the warnings. In fact, just last year our state of Colima was on the list of those Mexican states lining the Pacific coast up to the US border with the most drug-related crimes. On an almost daily basis, as we are out and about along the busy Manzanillo boulevard, we see *la guardia nacional* (formerly *federales*) patrolling in their imposing black vehicles, with masked police standing ready with automatic weapons; we see convoys of military trucks hauling dozens of soldiers and armor, we see military helicopters circling the bays for hours on end. We go about our day.

Rarely does this drug news make the local paper, *El Correo*. If asked, our Roque does give us a heads-up on the latest narco raids reported on the local Spanish radio, but he usually follows up the news alert with a chuckle and says in so many Spanish words, "Don't worry. The shooting was over on that other street." Okay then, we won't, Mister Will and I agree halfheartedly. We stay alert in Mexico.

But, we can't help wonder: How is this concern that much different than the crime rates back home? The US is having its own fill of drug wars and gang violence; we can't point fingers. The killings in Chicago have been described in the news as an "epidemic." In Minneapolis, we absolutely would never consider a night-time stroll in some of our neighborhoods known for frequent gang shootings. And drug busts happen all too often here in our Midwest USA city. And there's more: It's the US, not Mexico, where we are witnessing an outbreak and escalation of hate crimes. Our land-of-the-free USA is in a social crisis. We stay alert in the US.

Unfortunately, it just so happens that our Minneapolis is at the north end of a main drug pipeline from Mexico, a drug route which stretches from the border city Laredo, Texas, our border crossing point, all the way to Canada. "The Narco Corridor," otherwise known as Interstate Highway 35, is the major drug artery into the US. Then there are the likes of us in our Toyota Highlander on that very road making our way back and forth to Manzanillo each year, with only occasional icy roads to concern us. But that's not to diminish the seriousness, only to point out the irony; our communities south and north share the drug problem. More on this edgy topic and Mexico's systemic police problems in Chapter 10: X Cultures.

Considering that health and safety issues are top concerns for those who head to Mexico each year, I decided to conduct my own little survey of sorts in our community of the Manzanillo area. I wanted to know more about this subset of folks like

Mister Will and myself who swear by life in Mexico, drug wars and all. Why do we supposedly put ourselves at risk? I typed out a list of fifteen questions and handed it out to friends and acquaintances. Certainly, I assumed, stories would be revealed to support the worrisome news back home. Certainly, someone would report a bad experience. But no, with the exception of one minor theft due to a misplaced purse, the answers instead cast light on good, heartwarming experiences. All of those surveyed responded that they intend to continue coming to Mexico. One put it this way: "as long as health permits." That's a great barometer, if you ask me. In other words, one's good health should be the forecaster and not the media.

Understandably, Mexico rated high for the obvious: consistent lovely weather and consistent low cost. But get this: the next factor overwhelmingly was the "love of the Mexican people" themselves—their devotion to family values, their work ethic, their openness and kindness to us from another country and culture, so near and yet so far.

Distant Neighbor, by Alan Riding, explores the Mexican cultures in an attempt to shed light on the complex and very different country just next door. Knowledge about our close neighbors brings understanding. That's how I see our travels too, always gaining understanding with a growing "love of the Mexican people." And now I wonder if back home in the US we might accept our Mexican immigrants with an openness and kindness, which, in turn, would cause them overwhelmingly to respond in a similar tone: "We love the American people!"

When Mister Will and I bought our Casa 4, we knew very little really about our surrounding community. What we did know, however, was our strong attachment to Mexico and its people; that was a given, and we had this opportunity to live among them and learn more. We were confident that strong relationships would follow, and they did. Community.

Chapter 10 - X Cultures

Lesson: Know Your Inquisitive Side

At first glance, the notion of an extended stay in Mexico raises questions that would compare our two cultures broadly: US and Mexico. However, the many occasions that Mister Will and I have spent time in Mexico, first in rural communities and then at the coast and then in between, have taught us a lot more in a specific sense. The experiences have taught us more about ourselves.

Naturally, it's the Spanish language and the Mexican history, religion, and customs that shape the cultural experience, and this is what we as foreigners strive to learn when we travel to Mexico. As my US/Mexican friend Sally points out, "Language is tied to culture. If you don't know the language, you will never fully understand the culture." The socioeconomic differences within Mexico offer up lessons too. And, in our case, as retired vacationers now in a sought-out tropical destination, we share this Mexico experience along with many others like us. Or not like us. That's why in this chapter, I will pass along observations about Mexicanos generally and Mexicanos the upper class, as well as observations about us who visit from the States and Canada. Then, a further microcosm of culture in Mexico: expats and snowbirds.

At the Mercy of Language and Culture

Travel is a sure-fire method to shake up the senses and inevitably test us when we are out of our comfort zone. But that's a good thing, so the experts on healthy living say. I'd have to add...a good thing so long as those tests of travel flexibility don't raise havoc with our blood pressure. I'm thinking of scenarios like these: "What do you mean...our luggage is lost?" Or, "I don't understand what they are saying about our passports... Someone, please help!" But a gentle expanding of our comfort zone seems a welcome exercise, like the good feeling after a physical workout at the health club. Ah, refreshed.

That said, the distinction of setting up a house in a faraway foreign place, as opposed to a short getaway vacation here within our borders, might push the limits. Who could imagine all of the challenges? Are you ready to take it on?

Age experts tell us, "Get out of your comfort zone." Author Dinty W. Moore, while on a five-week course in Madrid, wanted "'to escape the role of tourist observer...to live the day-to-day life in someplace unknown to feel part of the place." Experience a different culture. Moore suggests "being at the mercy of language and custom." That strikes a bold chord. "Being at the mercy..." is humbly accepted by those of us who could use a few more lessons in speaking the language and understanding the culture. Mercy suggests leniency.

In Mexico, Mister Will and I depend on that leniency as we sputter out our makeshift conversations, hoping the locals will get our intended meaning and even help us along with our words. Then too, those conversations might just be about rather important business dealings, as in condo matters...as in pesos owed...as in owners who are not timely with their payments...as in hey, the condo gas tank needs to be replaced.. And we most certainly could use a tutorial on Mexican business protocol, if such a paper exists for us foreigners. We Americanos are at their mercy. We need leniency. But true, it's our fault for our ethnocentric tendencies; we should do better, and we know this. After all, it's their country, and we are the visitors. So in Mexico, we remain at the mercy of language and custom.

Naturally, over the many years in Mexico, Mister Will and I have learned a bit of Spanish: nouns mostly, and a few verbs which, of course, require that tough part: conjugation. The Spanish words we manage to put together in sentence form certainly are basic, unrefined, and sketchy. No matter, Mister Will and I aren't afraid to share what we know, however it comes out, just to communicate with the locals. That willingness on our part just to try was instilled in us decades ago when we first traveled to Mexico on a short-term mission. Before our departure, a wise world traveler, a missionary by vocation, schooled us on the rewards of experiencing another culture. He suggested that a person can travel the world, but until he has traveled that last eighteen inches...the distance between two people conversing...the person hasn't really experienced the new culture at all. "So speak up," he encouraged, "no matter how few words you know. Make mistakes. Show that other person you are trying." We took this advice to heart and struggle on with our Spanish. Perhaps we should switch our focus from language "barrier" to language "link."

Those nouns I mention have multiplied over the years as we have learned on the go, as needed. For instance, in the early years at the mission, we needed those words for work and church. The Spanish words that we followed along with on our song sheets stuck with us, as well as the Spanish lyrics so dramatically sung by strolling mariachis. As we traveled the cities, we soon learned the words for bus, car, hotel, room, restaurant, menu, tourist, all easy, as it turns out, because they are close cognates in English (*autobus, carro, hotel, restaurante, menu, turista)*). At the coast, we came to know the words for beach, sunset, whale, swimming pool. And in any of these locations, of course, we learned the words for breakfast, dinner, market, beer, colors, days of the week, months, numbers, any number of foods, and the most well-received...greetings.

Mexico's formal greeting, whether it's morning, afternoon, or evening, is engrained in all, whether laborer or professional, for each and every encounter. *Buenos dias...Buenas tarde... Burenas noche...*usually followed with "How are you?"...*Como estas?* and a handshake or, if appropriate, a light kiss, *beso,* on the cheek. And the conversation proceeds only after that polite exchange. Don't you agree, this sets a positive tone? And no matter the size of group addressed, this exchange is one-on-one until everyone has been suitably greeted. Imagine that sort of formality here in the States. Ours is more of a shorthand greeting, as in "Hey," a nod of the head, or simply no greeting at all.

Mexico condo living has its own set of useful business words, which certainly we as foreigners who own property should know in Spanish. Listen up, you potential buyers. Basic words like these go a long way: owner, renter, meeting, budget, estimate, contractor, taxes, bills, pay, buy, sell, attorney, court...and let's not forget the words for everyday repair and maintenance issues. Given the nature of these business dealings...at times not entirely chummy...those polite greetings I mentioned are ever so important. We as foreigners need to slow down, think about the broad picture of cultural relations, and put our best selves forward toward peaceful negotiations. Be polite. Then everyone leaves the meeting with a sense of self-respect and a notion that the particular issue will be resolved. Maybe, maybe not, but at least everyone is civil.

My Spanish usage to date has relied on what I call "the word tumbler." When I need to convey a message, I simply pull words from my personal collection, like my own little mental dictionary, then hobble them together with some gestures on my part for the verb action, or I might even know the verb form but only in the present tense. Fine, good enough, I think. This approach suffices most often. Still, I can do better, so I study a bit at least before we are headed to Mexico again. And quite naturally while we are in Mexico, words or phrases pop up that stick. Seeing the word spelled out often reveals a connection to English, as in *escalera* for stairway. Easy to associate with escalator, right? Here again, I suggest carrying a notepad and pen at all times.

So Mister Will and I cross that geographic border between Texas and Mexico, the Rio Grande, at least knowing this communication handicap, which we will have for our next few months. Communicating with our neighbors to the south requires hard work, so why not loosen up and play the language game. Both sides learn and even laugh, especially over the everyday communications, the tricky hurdles of syntax and idioms. Take, for example, an everyday conversation ordering breakfast: even a simple back and forth with a waiter about "eggs, over-easy" can be frustrating because that particular cooking preference apparently isn't part of Mexican culinary heritage or doesn't translate exactly. Time and time again, the eggs come to the table sunny-side-up. To avoid a convoluted ordering process, even to include an acting out of flipping an egg, and later to be served the unsatisfactory eggs, I give up and order *"revuelto"* scrambled. Recently sharing this language barrier with our Roque, we learned the phrase he uses: *"Huevo estrellado,"* roughly meaning "smashed egg." And that worked as to a fried egg, at least. But if it's a flipped egg you want, the word is *"volteado."* And if you prefer not too well done, then add, *"medio cocido."* You see the struggle, the energy required. But by simply asking a local, we solved the word mystery, and as a bonus, we gain a newfound respect from our Mexicano friends who see us trying really hard. That's human. So Mister Will and I give our language skills a go whenever we have that certain energy, but sometimes we just smile and go along with what is said... *"Si, si."*

The rewards we *gringos* are after—the climate, the colors, the music, the slower state of being that we find in Mexico—those rewards somehow ease the day-to-day challenges of this language barrier. We can feel at one with the locals swaying to the music, without needing to say a word. After so many years now, we do see that any language barrier actually breaks down with just minimal effort on our part. And the minimal effort at least brings smiles, and rather than a barrier, we see that link. The link then is another reward and part of the package with a cultural immersion in Mexico. Trust me on this and accept the challenge: Go that last eighteen inches.

On the Light Side: Mexico's Infrastructure

Here I'll throw in some basic advice on services in Mexico that, honestly, to me, shouldn't be so...so, let's say, outdated. A traveler ought to be prepared. After all, I reason, Mexico is just across the border from us...the USA, big super power, highly technologically advanced, industrialized nation that we are. But I'm confounded because just across the border sits Mexico, basically a developing country. We travelers from the privileged north don't know any better when it comes to escaping to the wonderful warm climate of Mexico. Perhaps in our light-headedness to get away, we assume we will have those basic services and conveniences from home such as reliable mail delivery and fully functional bathroom facilities, as we have been accustomed to our entire lives. No and no in Mexico.

Slower Than Snail Mail

In my humble opinion, Mexico's mail service should not to be taken seriously, as in trusting that whatever I send in the mail will reach its destination and in a matter of days, not weeks. Mexico's very slow and unreliable mail delivery seems to me more of a novelty. I don't know the reason, but mail as we know it here in the US doesn't happen in Mexico. "Why the heck doesn't Mexico figure it out?" is my standard frustration. "We are only a border away." Here at home, whenever the USPS increases the cost of a stamp, I welcome it—it's that good.

Apparently, a revamped department, Servicio Postal Mexicano, took effect in the mid-eighties in an effort to modernize Mexico's mail system, but from our experience, Mister Will and I will continue to advise, "Don't trust it." We have experimented on various occasions by sending a letter or postcard from Mexico to someone at home who is on notice to watch for it. About three weeks later, they happily report, "Yes, it arrived." So, the mail does finally get there...usually. The speed of delivery, we assume, is similar if sent in reverse—from home to Mexico—but somehow, somewhere, in that route after crossing the border, mail often gets lost or hung up at a dead end. Let's just say we have never considered mailing anything of value or importance to a Mexican address without at least requesting a return receipt, and even at that, we know that the return receipt will be weeks away. In one instance, we mailed, by certified return receipt, our trust payment to the Mexican bank. The bank claimed never to have received it, so then we were forced into a lengthy process with the bank to start all over again and rewrite our check. Where did the first one land?

One explanation for the unreliability, at least generally, just might be that many Mexican residences do not have a mailbox or mail slot, which means the mail carrier then has no choice but to drop the letter or package on the ground anywhere in the vicinity of the address. Quickly you can picture the fate of that delivery in the case of a swift breeze or an inquisitive dog. Only in recent years has our Posada del Sol offered a mailbox at the front gate, and that was only because one of our gringo neighbors took the initiative to buy one—not easy to find, by the way—and have it mounted. Until then, mail could be found strewn on the walkway inside our gate. Even now with the box, the mail carrier often continues the old practice.

Paying for utilities resorts to an old practice as well, with customers paying directly at the utility offices. With the postal service as it is, who would trust that the payment via the carrier reached the utility on time or in a suitable condition? And that assumes your payment is dropped in a bona fide mail drop—we assume the local post office—with the correct postage. No, we drive to each utility, stand in line with our *pesos*, and make our payment for the month as do the majority of locals. Now, interestingly, some services have online capability, which of course, completely leapfrogs that whole mail carrier tradition. I say good for the up and coming young Mexicanos, but that's not doable for us foreigners with no Mexican bank accounts, so we continue to wait in long lines and pay in cool *pesos*.

All this said, I have read posts on the internet from expats in various Mexican cities that suggest their experience in receiving mail, while slow, is very dependable. Hmm, the thought occurs: Might they be that upper class living in a gated community? Just speculation. I know too that many locals lease a box at the post office, which certainly eliminates the problem of misplaced deliveries out in the wild. This leased box idea could be the answer if deliveries were expected, as in an ongoing business, and the stay in Mexico would be something more than the three months that Mister Will and I have chosen to be in Mexico each year. Otherwise, we would be running needless circles to the post office to find nothing in the box...remember, the delivery time hovers at three weeks.

In the case of important papers, medicines, well, whatever it is that is imperative to receive, a delivery service such as DHL or, some say, UPS or FedEx, is the logical, superior choice of shipment, although expensive. Mister Will and I used DHL in 2004 when sending our signed purchase agreement to a lawyer in Manzanillo. No problem there. However, on another occasion, when receiving a package in Mexico delivered by DHL, we needed to learn the location of the DHL office; the package we were expecting turned up not at the location nearest our address but down the road in another community. This retrieval required *mucho* effort and perseverance on our part. Just make sure the sender selects the closest office.

Recently, we were set to wonder about shipments bigger than, say, our correspondence and papers after hearing a story from our friends about a twisted, complicated delivery of two boxes. Our Wisconsin friends, ever so patient and easy-going, waited over two hours at the customs center only to be directed to the downtown site miles away. Another long wait on a hot day. When that effort was unsuccessful, they returned on another day accompanied with their Spanish-speaking friend in hopes of clarifying the issue; after all, a command of Spanish seems a prerequisite when dealing with Mexican customs. Apparently, a couple of visits more, and still no boxes. You must understand that any one of these trips by car or taxi in the traffic in a tropical climate and the accompanying endless waiting in line can wipe out even the hardiest foreigner. But that's what we do. The boxes finally showed up for our friends, but not in Manzanillo and not that season...it was at the doorstep of their home in Milwaukee that spring, and now seriously soggy from a heavy downpour that day. The contents of the boxes didn't make the long journey again; instead, our friends found a destination for the contents right there in Milwaukee. Four hundred used golf balls: that's what it was that they had intended for their Mexican golf buddies—that's what didn't make it through customs.

Fortunately for us, Mister Will and I have not had to stake our life on a delivery from home, as in a delivery of medications prescribed by our doctor. We have known of those who do just that. No thanks for me. The most common practice of course is to bring along whatever stash of pills will carry you through the stay. Forget packing that extra shirt and make room for more pills. For the exploring and adventuresome sorts, a generic equivalent of medications often can be found in Mexico and at a savings too. Smooth healthy traveling, especially in retirement, requires some footwork.

When suitable, our visitors coming from home have been a welcome messenger service for us. In the case of just "wants" from home, they have kindly packed along our favorite magazines, dark chocolate (when it wasn't to be found in Mexico), and even our natural peanut butter (when it wasn't to be found in Mexico). And we use visitors when sending mail *back* home. If not our own visitors, I find someone traveling back to the States, no matter where in the States, who will carry my letter back to their home and then drop it in any US mailbox. I think of it as Mexican pony express. Of course, this pony express system only works if I find a traveler going back to the States at the particular time when I have a letter. No matter, I always pack with me a sheet of US stamps for such occasions.

When Mister Will and I choose this Mexican way of life each year, in addition to the language barrier, we accept the limitation of living in a foreign country without our customary mail services for those three or four months. Our trusty US Mail and US Parcel Post can only do so much when up against an encumbered, outdated Mexican postal system and overzealous Mexican customs agents.

But a bright spot emerges, at least to satisfy our consumer habits while away. Two words: Amazon Mexico. It works.

Sometimes Not So Tidy

Now this gets a little messy...the general inattention to litter and the not-up-to-par bathrooms can pose a problem for some travelers. For lack of a better word, I'll use "uneasiness" in describing the foreigner's take on orderliness and plumbing in Mexico. The culture of Mexican breaks in a big way from our sanitary standards back home. Let's face it: Mexico is a bit loose in trash management and lavatory standards. That's not to say that Mexico isn't neat and orderly in other areas, as in impeccably laundered and stylish clothes, oh my—even jeans reveal a pressed seam. Trees are well groomed, walkways swept, floors mopped daily. We foreigners observe these details and take note as we ride the buses and walk the neighborhoods for an authentic feel of Mexican life.

But let me weigh in on these other areas that can dismantle an unknowing new visitor to lovely Mexico. Better to be prepared. I can imagine that the trash problem had its beginnings with the inescapable plastic bags and bottles that infiltrated the country some forty years ago without an adequate refuse system to handle the throwaways or to educate the population on the consequences. The lavatory problem, well, my guess is that modern sewer systems just don't extend much beyond the large cities. The country's infrastructure seems poorly lacking, with vast areas of rural communities and no tax base for community services. The low daily wage of the Mexican laborer sadly works to the benefit of foreigners, as well as wealthy Mexicans.

From this country-wide litter problem to a country-wide inadequacy in plumbing, Mexico challenges those of us zealots for neat and clean. Orderliness and sanitation, I learned from childhood, are next to godliness, so logic would dictate that my good Minnesota parents, bless their souls, would have been miserable in Mexico. And that might be you too. Mexico has a wild west streak about it.

In recent years, harnessing the litter problem has made great leaps forward in the cities and especially in tourist areas. One can imagine the marketing for potential resort areas: Yes, city planners, your community too will benefit from vacationers if you just clean up your act. And it's not just international tourism which has helped Mexico, but Mexican tourism has become even more important. In our city of Manzanillo, we see huge numbers of Mexican families vacationing over the holidays in our coastal climate.

Back in the eighties I vividly recall my disgust at a Mazatlán beach where first I had to sidestep a swath of washed-up debris before reaching the ocean's edge. Mazatlán now is cleaned up, modern, and slick. Our city of Manzanillo has been transformed before our eyes, one year to the next, especially when the port was expanded and visiting cruise ships became a reality. Our beach now has a regular clean-up crew. Trash bins can be spotted on nearly every block. The port center has been updated with fresh paint and shaded walkways.

Even green initiatives are making a presence in the *supermercados*, with cloth shopping bags for sale. One *supermercado* actually has stopped the use of plastic bags, and if the customer has no cloth bag in tow, the bagger retrieves a cardboard box from packing. Still, for the masses of shoppers, plastic bags persist at an astounding rate, far greater, we have observed, than in our state of Minnesota. Even one item, say, a bottle of Coke, will be bagged unless you rush to wrestle it free. Paper bags are nowhere in Mexico. And, to our knowledge, the ubiquitous, clingy poly bags still have no recycle option. Just as the indestructible white plastic chairs infiltrated the Mexican countryside at the dawn of plastic-making, the life of the plastic bags seems to be infinite. But for the start of environmental steps so far, we cheer: *Mexicanos,* power to Mex Green! Noteworthy too is less waste in Mexico as compared to the US. Mexicans tend to use everything until it is not useful anymore and then try to find another way to make it useful. Reduce and Reuse: They have that down.

Yet alas, the disappointing bathrooms. Mexico's idea of bathroom conveniences still after all these years takes my…well…breath away. "Really?" I mutter when I experience "The Experience" that first time back in Mexico after a year away. Like maybe one of these years, Mexico's plumbing facilities culture will change. Please note that what I have here to say mostly applies to stops along our road trip in Mexico and to everyday establishments, not necessarily to franchise hotels and restaurants. Mostly. A good plumbing delivery system, up to code as we know it back home…that could be the tie breaker for new visitors to the country. "Oh, but what would that cost? a Mexican citizen might gasp. We foreigners need to be reminded that the minimum wage in Mexico is $10.00 per day, and some locals cannot afford any indoor plumbing, much less plumbing up to American standards.

So, foreigners best be knowledgeable and know what to expect. Not only are many of the public toilets incapable of handling any form of paper, which necessitates that it is disposed in a waste basket, but *papel* generally is only available from an attendant at the door (usually a man by the way, which is humiliating for both of us, it seems to me). Here he perches, handing out only a few thin sheets for a fee of five *pesos* (about 25 cents). This setup also ensures a mostly clean bathroom. Sometimes *papel* isn't available at all; this is when your own tissue packet proves its worth. The faucets only function with cold water, and paper towels are nonexistent. Make that toilet seats too—basically not there. Soap might be in the form of powdered detergent in a cup, or a scrap of bar, or nothing at all. Versions of this scenario are throughout rural Mexico, especially and in the outskirts of the cities. Upscale restaurants and hotels have vastly improved facilities, some even modern classy in high-end tourist areas. But the takeaway is this: A traveler savvy to Mexico will always, always have on hand a packet of tissues, a sanitizer, and a sense of humor.

The irony to me is that restrooms are known as "*sanitarios.*" Once at a crowded, lively bar, the waste basket in the *sanitario* was heaped full and overflowing to the floor, and soap was absent. The worst *baño* in my Mexican travels did not have running water at all, so the choice then was to fill a bucket at the door for flushing. But to be fair, that was at a beach restaurant. And to be fair, let's not forget that back home in the US and Canada, outhouses are the answer in our own north woods camping; campers look at it like getting back to nature. Could it be that hand sanitizers were inspired by these conditions.

Long before Mister Will and I began our Mexico stretch of travel, we learned something about this cultural distinction as to bathroom hygiene when we fostered a Vietnamese girl in our home for a year. She, the foreigner in our strange new culture, found it extremely difficult to accept our standard of throwing waste tissue in the toilet. This I learned after weeks of emptying smelly waste baskets. Who would have predicted that Mister Will and I would learn a cultural lesson in our own home from this eighteen-year-old and then revisit that lesson years later in Mexico? We here from our privileged homes in *el norte* need constant reminders that the majority of the world does not operate under nor conform to any semblance of the Uniform Plumbing Code as we know it here in the US. But with a little commonsense personal hygiene habits when traveling to developing countries, we can avoid any lurking bad germ manifesto.

When Mister Will and I worked in the mountains with the Mazahuan people, our Mexican facilitator/missionary advised us on the ill-conceived merits of outhouse projects in rural areas. Logically, we thought, the poor people just needed our help and resources to build these structures—then obviously they won't need to use the great outdoors for such purposes. Our facilitator told us otherwise: The perfectly respectable outhouses constructed by mission workers from *el norte* were never used for the intended purpose...instead, the fine structure was used to store corn for their tortillas. "Why," the people asked, "would we use this good space for a *baño*? We have the open fields for our *baño.*" This explanation was so outside our reality that it took us aback; you can see us with that blank look of disbelief. "Really?" But a deeper look at the culture of these rural towns brought us around to see their rationale. Yes, of course, their corn is their sustenance, their livelihood. So we learned: *tortillas* reign over structured bathrooms in rural Mexico.

Such had been our on-site cultural training when Mister Will and I ventured further in our quest for foreign adventure, even to own a place in Mexico. My personal lesson in flexibility to pass along? When someone such as myself can be trained to dispose of toilet tissue, not in the toilet but in a basket alongside, and to do this and still maintain a love for the culture, that says something about acceptance. My German/Norwegian upbringing taught me a hyper-alertness to germs and anything unsightly, or even out of place, in a bathroom. So the basket alternative to risky plumbing has been my biggest cultural challenge in Mexico, by far. Even our own Casa 4 was not connected to the city sewer system for our first ten years, thus requiring the unsightly basket. Need I even detail my embarrassment when we had guests? I applauded the day when that first paper went down. Mexico *is* progressing at a rapid rate these days, with modern plumbing in the cities and tourist areas, but this other scenario of toilet culture is usually just a street away.

Comunicado Advances

Reflecting on these basic services, which we all have accepted as normal back home, I'll add yet another to the list, not quite as dramatic but still a challenge: international phoning. This topic I'm including even though now cell phones make long-distance life easier by a long shot. The problem really is landline phoning. Mister Will and I seem forever holding fast to our landline in Mexico simply because it's what we know: a comfortable relic, no doubt. Those decades ago when we worked at the mission, phoning really was out of the question, either because of the high cost or the lack of transmission. Any time that phone lines were installed in those outlying areas, the lines might disappear overnight because the locals had a better use for that copper. I recall finally walking to a rural settlement where we found a phone booth for calling home to our kids and my very old dad. So Mister Will and I fall naturally into this hesitation about phoning. And it's a fact that even now a long-distance landline call is expensive. And from what we hear, cell phone calls *to us* from the US, if not on an international phone program, can be expensive.

Our more modern, up-to-date friends seem to get along just fine with their various slick phone plans from home, as in unlimited texts, so-and-so reduced rate for calls, blah, blah, but for us slightly behind, our cell phone coverage is cut at the border—another one of those services that abruptly stops. So, over the years we have come to rely on a computer-based call system that works just fine most of the time and is only a few cents per minute; we only have to at add dollars when the balance of minutes runs low. But it is a little clunky as opposed to just picking up the phone and dialing. Our Manzanillo, now so modern, does offer cell phones on a monthly plan, handy for us travelers. Just ask our friend Betty, an eighty-year-old who overcame the obstacles in purchasing the thing and managing the in-person, wait-in-a-long-line monthly renewals, all in Spanish, and now swears by the convenience and minimal cost. She phones with ease. Mister Will and I should make this our next logical step in Mexican twenty-first century communications. Meanwhile, our go-to for best communications has been, and I bet will continue to be, basic email. We tell our family and friends, if you need to reach us, don't call, email. Or text.

The inconveniences and uneasiness that go hand in hand with these cultural differences are a reality for anyone visiting Mexico and especially staying long term. After the shock-and-awe reaction, we foreigners think it through, collect our thoughts, and inevitably come back to focus on those basic intangible rewards we know are waiting for us in Mexico: the climate, the colors, the music, the laid-back state of being. We wish for these things after too long in our buttoned-down communities in the north. Needing to break out, we hurry to be immersed again into the very different foreign culture of Mexico, bad plumbing and all, and to experience the very different change in ourselves.

On the Dark Side: Mexico's "Bite" and More

Certainly Mexicans must know that theirs is a culture to be envied, where social beats out schedules every time. They must wonder at our hurried behavior, with our fixation on clocks. You might notice that a majority of the Mexicans do not wear a watch. Mexico's playful colors and music seem to support and accentuate this focus on social relationships. Who wouldn't ease back and take more time to enjoy the moment if, say, engrossed in vivid hues of the warm outdoor surroundings, with background rhythms so lyrical in three/four time? And where relationships come first, families naturally benefit. Mexico is a family-based culture. What we at first see as a rambunctious group of Mexicans disturbing our peace and quiet at the pool is actually an extended family with all age groups lively engaged. I want to join in! Now in that light, we are more the same.

Unfortunately, the differences that sell newspapers are *not* so enviable: the drug cartels, the corrupt police force, the unstable government. These are the topics front and center when our family and friends, only intending to help, ask us about Mexico. "So, what is it like there in Mexico...any problems where you go? You know...the problems we see on the news channel...problems with safety?"

Mexico for centuries has had this stigma of dark mystic. In *Distant Neighbors,* author Alan Riding attempts to put light on the enormous divide existing between our cultures. He claims if

Mexico loses its originality and identity, "it loses its way....What will survive is Mexico." And that likely is what Mister Will and I find so intriguing about the place. It remains an original.

Many from north of the border tend to be put off by Mexico's challenges and risks. How much easier, the rationalizing goes, to stay put within our comfy borders. Closer to doctors is one of the top reasons. A character in Harriet Doerr's *Consider This Señora* was tempted to buy property in Mexico but "was restored to clear thinking" when his wife asked if he had lost his mind. She could only ask, "Live in a place where you can't drink the water, eat the food, understand the exchange, or trust the police?" Bear in mind, this story was set in the 1980s, predating the escalation of drug wars confronting Mexico today. So, add drug wars to that list.

El Chapo, the notorious Mexican drug lord who escaped prison not once, but twice, is something of a folk hero in Mexico, at least in his hometown of Culiacan near the Pacific coast. No matter that he is responsible for thousands of brutal killings, his mere support of youth soccer teams and other community services in the town where he grew up somehow elevates him above the law. Townspeople know exactly who finances the local parks. Money laundering comes to mind. The locals turn an eye. That certainly says something about the disconnect with how we North Americans view our travel to Mexico, knowing that the likes of El Chapo are behind the scenes.

Aside from the effect of the Denzel Washington movie *On Fire*, which we just happened to catch on our motel room television the night before crossing the border, our answer has been a resolute "Yes, we feel safe!" But here's the thing about that movie: To me, the unnerving happenstance of that movie on that date at that hour could only be a warning as clear as a tornado siren back home. As if speaking to us directly right there from the television, this was a last-minute alarm of sorts for out-of-touch northerners like ourselves: "Hello there you two from Minnesota, heading down to Mexico...listen up!" You need to understand, we were a bit nonchalant in our headiness with this high adventure and absolutely needed a not-so-gentle reminder of possible brutality and/or kidnapping and, at the very least, the possibility of bad-guys-in-the-vicinity now that we were here at the border, that very thin line between the US and scary Mexico. Those hardcore scenes shot in Nuevo Laredo were mightily disturbing. I had little sleep that night.

For the most part, we do not question our safety, and we roam the country quite freely. But, let's face it, kidnapping in Mexico, whether fact or fiction, always raises concerns; might we foreigners end up at the wrong place at the wrong time? Another movie about the drug war also has left a lingering chill. That movie is *Sicario*. With the realism of a documentary direct out of northern Mexico, the fictional story depicts an El Chapo character, ghoulish killings, and an intricate tunnel system beneath the border. The secondary, more heartfelt story, is the all-too-common plight of an everyday Mexican cop turned bad who leaves behind an impressionable young son. Viewers leave the theater in a dark daze. Perhaps Hollywood does a better job at grabbing our attention than the actual news reported.

That's the effect of good drama. So, it's acknowledged: Mister Will and I do take special note of news reports, travel warnings, and now, the latest movies on the subject of Mexico. But our answer remains "No!" And let's not forget the drama when friends and family warn. We halt our plans enough to access the big picture, the context, the perils...and then we strike out on the road again. All seems in proper perspective once more as we head out on our journey to our winter home, homed-in on a compass pointing due south.

Mister Will and I aren't unusual in accepting Mexico as it is. You can count on the response. Anytime a group of us North Americans are discussing the subject of the Mexican cartels as we exchange stories on our patios, the consensus remains: Hey, our cities back home are downright dangerous. What's the difference? Look at the death toll in Chicago, for example, or the north side of our very own Minneapolis. Our Canadian friends point out Vancouver. The unsettling effect of random violence in the US feels the same as the unsettling effect of drug violence in Mexico.

Maybe it's the drug cartel's style that's off-putting: lopping off heads. Bodies and/or body parts are dumped in strategic spots to send a message. Armored vehicles with masked police are routine in our city. Like the mafia wars back home, these drug cartels are all about power within the group. We just don't want to be caught in the middle, that's all.

So, we gringos, as we chat over our margaritas and *cervesas,* talk big about the dangers out there. What little news filters through the local papers we likely miss because we can't read Spanish well enough or because we just don't follow the news as we do back home. Oh, we do keep an eye on *Mexico Daily News,* the English edition, but basically, we fall into relax mode and simply place our trust in our own safe habits: We are not in bars late at night and do not buy drugs. Simple. "Let the drug guys fight it out," is the consensus.

The incidences about which we do have firsthand knowledge only raise our awareness, as in a warning "be aware of your surroundings." So we are. The drug news that comes to us is usually by word of mouth given our smallish community, so the facts as we understand them are not always reliable or complete. But it's what we go on. Here is a sampling from recent years: A dead body, decapitated, linked to a cartel, was discovered behind the local cinema. A narco raid, leaving one man dead, occurred in a small town just north of Manzanillo. In the town just farther up the road from our church a man was killed in a drug deal gone bad. Helicopters circled low in our neighborhood for a full two days when police were tracking two drug suspects. Cartels have infiltrated certain bars by coercing payments for safety. A local attorney dealing in money laundering was shot dead at a sidewalk café by a drive-by motorcyclist.

    The general warnings we hear banish driving in certain states along our Pacific coast corridor. The state of Guerrera, for instance, has been a troublesome spot so we avoided it and took a longer route when we drove to a writers' conference some seven hours away. This travel advice interestingly came from a market vendor who drove his strawberries to our Manzanillo from the state of Guerrero. I was glad for my bit of Spanish to ask the question.

    Many years ago the issue of corrupt police became personal. This was on the other coast of Mexico outside Cancún where two from our family were stopped in their rental car. They were escorted outside the city limits where the police leveraged a couple hundred dollars' worth of pesos before returning the passports. Frightening? Absolutely! Now we know that rental cars in tourist areas are a flag for an easy target.

    We know this police gig too with privately owned buses traveling across state lines in Mexico. On one of our mission trips in the nineties, the police stopped our bus, and it was only after a very lengthy negotiation with the Mexican driver and a handsome payment that we were on our way again. Our Mexican organizer friends just accepted this instance as a method by which police could make a little extra *dinero*. This, we learned, is Mexico. The term is *la mordida*: "the bite" of the traffic cop.

That bite is almost understandable after learning the plight of the Mexican traffic police: very low wages, with an understanding that he or she can supplement through bribes. The practice traditionally has been a way of Mexican life and is probably the most visible form of official corruption we see in Mexico. It works: Many drivers actually prefer to pay the *mordida* rather than the more expensive fine. Our US friend often retells his *mordida* story: When lost in Puerta Vallarta backstreets he was stopped for driving the wrong way on a one-way street. When the female cop threatened a hefty fine, our friend, who knew the drill and was in a particular hurry to meet his daughter at the airport, flashed several hundred pesos instead. That satisfied the cop, she forgave the ticket, and she in fact happily led him on his way...ironically still driving the wrong way on a one-way. Our experience was a bit different. Mister Will and I were confronted with a ticket when our car was parked slightly over a pedestrian crossing in downtown Manzanillo. Mister Will tried in fact to work the system too by offering this traffic cop, again a woman, payment on the spot. He did not want to deal with the details and time of paying the ticket in person at an unknown location. The policewoman, however, was above it: "*No, no, señor,*" she said, wagging her finger and with a stern face. She proceeded in writing the ticket.

We foreigners are fully aware that the bite will continue in Mexico, and we are fully aware that police corruption has extended far beyond traffic matters. It's Mexican reality. Still, in the case of a parking ticket, Mister Will and I did witness a cop who did *not* take the bite. More about the ticket and Mexico's system for collecting on these tickets in my chapter on driving.

The numbers? As for us in our own car with Minnesota plates, we have logged some 60,000 miles on Mexican roadways over twelve-plus years with zero incidences, well, except for the parking ticket. Zero. And zero is what we hear from our many US and Canadian friends and acquaintances who drive freely across the states of Mexico.

The Mexican culture is a spicy mix that, over time, becomes easier on the palate for some like us in *el norte* who continue to venture south despite the obstacles. Dare I say that after a touch of the *piquante* here and there, we have become accustomed to the hot, and even wait for it. The fact that dozens of *federales* showed up in Manzanillo this year simply stirred our attention enough to take particular notice, and sure enough, reports filtered through a restaurant owner confirmed that, yes, the cartels were in the neighborhoods. Shootings happened, bars threatened, establishments closed down. For us, a topic for happy hour. Perhaps we should wonder: What is in those drinks that eases our safety concerns?

But our usual relatively calm take on this unsettling, scary Mexico picture stems, I believe, from all the good we've seen thus far, the good that tips the balance. Without question, the firsthand instances that Mister Will and I reflect on *most* often when we are returning to Mexico are not those of drugs and killings and traffic bites, but instead are those of inspiration and hope in our Latino neighbors. Our firsthand experiences act as an antidote to any uneasiness we might have about the people across the border. For instance, the doctor in Morelia who came to our hotel room for a nominal charge on a busy weekend when I was overcome with vertigo on a long trip. The village women in El Naranjo who immediately came to my aid with home remedies of raw onion and cool water when I lay faint on the street with a bout of food sickness. The waiter in San Luis Potosi who sought us out late at night amid a busy street of hotels to return our travel bag containing irreplaceable papers, including passports. The woman in Manzanillo who bused into town on our behalf to return our internet modem inadvertently left behind as we hurriedly packed to go home, a sizable savings for us. The auto saleswoman who insisted I have her bracelet after I commented on its attractiveness. The innumerable patient Mexicanos waiting in lines with us at the bank, the grocery store, the utilities, the return counters, stepping in with a smile to help with Spanish. Like reviewing favorite snapshots, we remember.

Mexico's Upper Class

Mexico's new upper class is perhaps our least understood group, and these are the very Mexicans who are co-owners at Posada...our neighbors. Having immersed ourselves for years in the work of short-term missions in the high plateau villages northwest of Mexico City, we learned about Mexico's culture and rich heritage from the bottom up on the economic scale. Those native and *mestizo* peasants we worked alongside symbolized to us the heartbeat of Mexican life. We understood certainly that Mexico had its share of the world's very wealthy, but the vast majority were the rest, the very poor sprawled in the cities and tucked-in mountain villages.

As we began to tour the coastal vacation hotspots and the heavily populated inland cities, we encountered another category of Mexicans: the upper class. Each year that we have visited, the numbers have seemed to double. We see it in the development of upscale shopping malls, which seem strangely out of place when just across the street are locals selling from their *tienda* stalls, usually with small children underfoot or sleeping nearby in a hammock. The transformation has been astounding. Just twenty years ago our mission team was challenged to find suitable lumber for a playground. We made do at a scrapyard by salvaging old warped boards. Now, even in mid-size communities, a Home Depot is just down the street. And now, we have slick, modern shopping.

In our small role as visitors for a short time each year, we observe this upper class from a distance. Though these locals appear more like us, we sense a disconnect. Their high-end cars, the fashionable clothing, the latest in electronics, all come across like expenditures overextending a credit limit. Even their grocery carts heaped to the limit, then topped off with beach toys for the children, draw our attention. How can these Mexicans afford all this, we wonder in our narrow view from our highly industrialized nation.

Mister Will and I are much more likely to strike up a conversation with a Mexican laborer who knows little English than we might strike up a conversation with this more educated upper class who tend to know a good bit of English. Ironic? Our reluctance, of course, is our limited Spanish which is intimidating, but I would guess too that we are taken aback by the displays of wealth we see in this class. Might that aloofness we sense from these upper-class Mexicans just be that they see us as supremely wealthy ourselves. After all, we are the tourists jetting in for a holiday at their Manzanillo on the ocean. After all, they could reason, our three-month stay does require some financial wherewithal. And they must wonder, why aren't the foreigners' families with them? And, why, Patron Saint of Good Manners, are these foreigners always in a hurry? Have they no patience for proper greetings?

On the other hand, we from the north, in our world of Social Security and work pensions, have this sense of what's due. We have worked hard, saved, and carefully budgeted to enjoy our Mexico getaway—living the dream, as they say. And we hope our families will visit and catch the draw of Mexico too. As for our impatience and lax manners, we'll work on that.

In the intimate confines of our Posada del Sol where we as neighbors and co-owners share the pool, the beach, and any of the common spaces, we pick up on these differences in our cultures, front and center. This just might be the perfect study of side-by-side cultural behaviors. Setting aside for a minute all of the genuine goodness we see in our Mexican neighbors, in the spirit of lessons Mister Will and I have learned, I will elaborate on some of the, let's say, unruly behaviors in our tight condo setting. After all, you should be in the know if you are considering an investment such as ours. These behaviors seem out of place with the otherwise formal courtesies we see in the Mexican culture generally and, frankly, can quickly get under the skin. But this is a reality of Mexico condo living, a cross-cultural lesson in expanding what we choose to see.

When our Mexicano owners show up at our Posada del Sol, or when their extended family using those condo units show up, or when their friends using those condo units show up, we North Americans basically take cover. Their aggressive behavior in dominating all of the common areas leaves us speechless, in effect shocked that our quiet, orderly haven at Posada has been disrupted. From out of nowhere, it seems, they show up at the pool and common grounds, first one, then a couple, then a dozen fill the spaces that we have savored as our private quiet places. Suddenly we have to share...and share we do, however with a skeptical, territorial eye. What gives them the license, I wonder, to park their lounge chairs directly tight up against our patio walkway, causing us to step around or stay put? Why do they light up cigarettes directly in front of our open kitchen window? Why do they cut across our patio as a shortcut for any reason?

The fact that the Mexicans are in seemingly "our space" simply confounds us foreigners. While our tendency is to avoid all attention in this close setting for the peace and quiet in our

Posada space, theirs is quite the opposite. We slip in and out of the pool with little notice, move about quietly, keep our voices low and our music barely audible. Pianissimo. Like good library behavior.

So you see how our cultures collide. We observe a difference in parenting as well. Young Mexican children roam freely, we watch, into the pool, out of the pool, up and over tables, across other patios, up and down the walkways; all the while the permissive parents are engaged only on the fringe, perhaps. Oh, they are watching, but not necessarily coaching their children in proper social behavior at the pool, as in no long-term screaming, no chasing onto other patios, no undue splashing if someone might be sunning at pool's edge. Interestingly, after observing for some years, we see these unruly children mature into respectful and friendly young adults who, by the way, have a good command of the English language.

So it is, we experience unexpected, sometimes irritating sounds in our paradise *Mexicano*. If on the outside chance we North Americans do introduce music, say, from our private patios, we like to think it's tasteful for anyone else who might hear, and always, always toned down. Consider classical. Our former neighbor from the US played endless Cher...but toned down. One exception to this quiet politeness is when our domino group cranks up an old rock favorite for a sing-along, but really, that's it. After the tune and a nervous look around for anyone who might be disturbed, we turn it down. In the case of vacationing Mexicanos, at the very least one boom box with amped-up speakers blasts tunes for the entire area of pool and common grounds for hours on end. Consider pop Mexicano, old-time Mexicano, Frank Sinatra.

Also on the noise front, hollering from one side of the complex to the other is common, and even accepted, by the

Mexicanos, especially if signaling for assistance from Roque for, say, hauling pool chairs or buying cigarettes. Loudly: "Roque! Roque!" And he appears. Another common Mexican call for attention is a sharp but friendly whistle, which is subtle and, I find, more mannerly, and even endearing—sometimes like a bird call, someone stands at the locked gate to signal Roque.

And now about pets, which so easily translates to irritating noise. I understand that our Posada condo rules say something to the effect, "no pets." At least we foreigners agree on that, but who knows for sure, given our poor Spanish and the state of our condo documents. We commiserate about the lack of respect for rules...our English rules apparently. Nonetheless, the Mexicanos arrive with at least one dog in tow. Not one of us gringos speaks up when confronted with a dog visitor because, well, we want to be endlessly friendly. (We are still working on our Spanish greetings.) The issue is brought up in fact at our annual meeting, time and time again by one of us, but the Mexicanos know we have no enforcement. They acknowledge the comment, and the discussion turns to another topic.

In Posada bygone years, long, long ago, it was an Americano actually who always had her cat with her, so we hear. At least that pet was quiet. In recent years, the small-breed lap dog has become fashionable in Mexico, even those that fit in a purse. So, I suppose, our Mexican neighbors might argue that small is almost like no dog at all. *No problemo.* Yet it's these small yappy ones that get our attention when they are left unattended inside while the owners step out for the evening. Larger dogs too call Posada their vacation getaway...a police dog, a pit bull, well behaved, but really? We are always going to step out of their way, thank you.

In our open-air setting and close quarters, Mister Will and I in Casa 4 have no remedy but to put up with the lively *Mexicano* presence or leave. Generally, we cook up an excuse to vacate on an errand or two. This technique not only gets us away from the disruptions, but prompts us with our to-do list and brings us back refreshed...for at a later hour, the *Mexicanos* will be gathered for their mid-afternoon meal and the pool and quieter surroundings will be ours to enjoy.

But you know just where I'm heading with this cross-cultural confusion, the toss-up of norms, and my backpedaling: deep down, we from *el norte* envy our Mexican neighbors. It's true. Our pent-up, inhibited selves want out. Besides, it's exhausting to fuss and fume, to be the Posada police. What, after all, is the point of a restorative time away without a loosening of our collars? Intentionally or not, we build our own walls. If we could just once drop some of our northern European inhibitions, some of our preconceived notions on what's proper or not as in Emily Post etiquette, we might join in the party. We might bring out our boomboxes too and even stake our place at the pool. After all, we've been tapping our toes to their music all along. Amazing as it is to us, the unruly children now several years later have matured into respectful, thoroughly delightful young adults.

Amazing as it is to us, just a try at conversing with our Mexican neighbors leads to common ground and warm relationships. Who would guess that Mister Will and I would be invited to join in a game of dominos with one of these over-powering families? Well, there we were at the game table counting our points in Spanish. Might it be that a simple game can span our differences?

Others of Us: The Canucks

We are crazy-wild about our Canadian friends...but we went south to find them. Our first ever social interaction with our northern neighbors wasn't there in Canada, not in the US, but a couple thousand miles away in Mexico. And this wasn't until we were in our retirement years. I wish we had looked sooner.

Little did we know when our interest in Mexico piqued, that a south of the border experience would offer an expanded vocabulary in more than the Spanish language. New English words would come into play. Words now part of our vocabulary include: porridge (oats), chesterfield (sofa/couch/davenport), runners (running shoes), appies (appitizers), breaky (breakfast), toque (stocking hat), keener (a doer, as in he's a doer), and let's not forget those crazy British pronunciations, i.e., roof, project, begin, again, garage, creek (all slightly with a long sound). And the British spellings, which came onto my radar when my Canadian friend looked at part of my book *Gumption*; she insisted on changing the spelling of "pajama" to "pyjama." Aye! It's Canadian!

Just head south to Mexico, in the mid of winter, and you will find our northern neighbors, Canadians, lots of them. For us seeking all things cross cultural, this unfoldment has been a surprise gift. Not only do we immerse ourselves in Mexico, but as a side course in cultural studies, we observe and learn from our Canadian friends and are better US citizens for it.

And learn we do. As a starter, finally we now can list the ten Canadian provinces and actually know where they are on the map. In contrast to that modest achievement, our Canuck friends boast to know not only our states but the capitols, the industries, the landmarks. Why is it that they have studied more about us than we about them? They have traveled extensively in the US, read our national newspapers, and they are well versed in our banking and politics. Our Toronto friend likes to remind us that they stay in tune because, of course, much of their commerce and finance depends upon the US, the dominant international power. Not vice versa as much. But that Toronto friend also likes to point out that the US system has deep flaws where the choice of the people isn't always consistent with the political process. Healthcare comes to mind, and on this, we agree. But hold it there, fair Canadian...don't step too hard on our sensitive US toes.

In one of our happy-hour talk fests solving world problems and inevitably comparing our two countries, I asked lightheartedly, "So what is it that you say about us US folks? Come on...tell us the truth." We had been sharing a laugh over a Canadian joke on tipping in restaurants (What's the difference between a Canadian and a canoe? ...A canoe tips...hee, hee), a joke in fact told by one of our Canadians. The answer to my question was anything but funny: "The US is too capitalistic! Everyone is out for himself!" Whoa. For me, that response put a whole new light on my national pride. Really? You mean to say that even our close buddies there in Canada wonder about our inner morals when it comes to the economy? Are we from the US really so full of ourselves and narrowly focused on getting ahead?

The comment stood without much comeback from us, just startled looks. Much later I was still wrestling with the sting of that comment. "Wait," my defensive, baby-boomer-self wanted to say, "weren't we from the US taught our whole lives that free enterprise and entrepreneurship are the strength and foundation of America? Aren't these the principles that draw so many from all across the planet to our land of the brave?"

Here again, generalizations are risky, even when joking about tipping habits. But in a good way too, we generalize about all of those qualities we notice, as in: Canadians are proper, stoic, hard working, amiable, well-mannered, loyal, adventuresome, and always on time and even early. I love the proper behavior. We're hoping they can generalize too about us, in a good way

So we in the US can learn a thing or two from our neighbors to the north, whether we are ordering our medicines online from Canadian sources or learning from Canada's even keel in welcoming immigrants. We in the US, in our lofty role as leader of the free world, seem to be more insecure than powerful, more anxious than confident. When the US was in the throes of bash politics with the Clinton vs. Trump campaign, a Canadian media campaign was born: "Tell America It's Great Again." Our Canuck friends felt our pain.

Others of Us: Expats

To my ear, the term "expatriate" has a mysterious, exciting, even romantic ring to it. Like studying abroad, but more. Maybe my husband and I qualify for that tag, but then I'm not sure if our three months a year meets the criteria. Dictionary definitions range from 1) a person taking up residency in another country, 2) a person who lives outside their native country, 3) living abroad, and then the dark meaning, 4) exiled. Most certainly we love our USA and will never give up our roots in Minnesota, but we do proudly announce to our friends and family that Mexico *is* our residence for those three winter months each year. Still, we do not refer to ourselves as expats. Likewise, we do not refer to ourselves as "snowbirds," but more on that later. Are we a different breed?

The expats that come to mind for us are the Americans and Canadians who live in Mexico nearly year-round and who are engaged in a business, whether realty, food service, construction contracting, renting, teaching, preaching, the arts. They tend to live in beautifully designed homes of their own. Also qualifying might be those who are just the opposite of engaged; they simply are drop-outs, some with questionable pasts, choosing a laid-back, out-of-touch lifestyle in temperate Mexico. Either way, these long-term foreigners in Mexico are the ones we call "expats."

Expats seem to be dialed down a notch or two in their temperament. Whether carrying on a business or carrying on that laid-backness, they project contentment. Maybe that's what a slower pace can do. "No-hurry, no-worry" appears to be the mantra.

Others of Us: Snowbirds

Lastly, I bring up this subculture which, to me, gets too much press: "snowbirds." It's true that thousands of Americans and Canadians flock to Mexico simply to avoid winter in the north. No denying it, the warm tropical winds in lieu of blustery cold can do wonders for a northern soul. I'm just not fond of the term because, of course, snowbirds almost exclusively are retirees, which of course correlates to those of us in our senior years. In other words, "snowbirds" sounds old and, frankly, boring, like muzak piped in a department store.

To be fair, the term "snowbirds" for those escaping to Mexico encompasses a wide variety of folks who simply like warmer weather and...a critical distinction...are adventuresome sorts. Warmer weather is easy enough to find in Florida or Arizona or Hawaii, where language isn't a factor and where that dark mystic I mentioned isn't hovering. Choosing Mexico, on the other hand, requires an additional level of curiosity. Our friends and acquaintances are 100% sold on Mexico and all its issues, the good and the not so good. A hardy sort.

The wide variety of snowbirds is seen in the choice of accommodations, from high-rise luxury condos, to modern fourplexes, to single-family dwellings, to simple older beach apartments, to travel-trailer communities, to single rooms at old hotels. We fall somewhere in the middle with our modest Casa 4 from the sixties. Whether owners or renters, we snowbirds are alike: We love our Mexico.

Obviously, the luxury of time to get away for a long stretch and the luxury of savings to make it happen don't often present to young, everyday, working individuals—especially true for parents still raising children. There are the occasional young savvy travelers who do make it happen. We have met couples toting young children along, all with backpacks and a healthy glow. They always come across as wise beyond their years. Those children inevitably will continue through life learning in foreign places and becoming richer for the experiences. And we have met young couples creatively gearing their jobs to be adaptable offsite. The internet suddenly expanded the workplace from brick-and-mortar office to world. And we have met young teachers and entrepreneurs who simply take a sabbatical. What better than quality time spent in totally new surroundings to find fresh perspective?

So the allure of a warm climate certainly is a draw, but I for one will always wince if pegged a snowbird. The suggestion that Mister Will and I are of the group that automatically flee for a warmer climate, *just because*—that we ended up in Mexico to avoid Minnesota winters and muddy springs—doesn't give complete perspective about us and likely many more like us. Our journey started with a simple interest in living in another culture. Interestingly, that interest, which began for the two of us well before we even knew each other, was triggered back to President Kennedy's initiative in the sixties: the Peace Corps. Then, in the

1980s, when Mister Will and I became a couple, that interest in other cultures intensified, as if somehow in our earlier lives we had missed out. For us, opportunities arose; first it was Haiti, then Mexico's highlands, then finally our Casa 4 on the Pacific. Might we fall into an entirely new category, for instance, "Alternative Mexico"? We could shorten it and be totally hipster with "Alt-Mx," as in "Yah, we're the Alt-Mx group." Hmm, I like the sound of that. Eyebrows might raise.

Mexicanos of course are enticed to travel north to experience our culture, but it's the jobs they are after, not the climate and certainly not our hurried pace. Often they are the ones "restored to clear thinking" and return to their beloved Mexico to reclaim their rich heritage, trading better pay for better lifestyle. And in recent years, with less economic benefit in the north and more opportunities in Mexico, lower numbers are setting out for *el norte*. We have encountered Mexican laborers, waiters, bankers, and realtors who learned their good English in the US or Canada and now have happily returned to their families in Mexico. Why wouldn't they? For us, having lived this culture, even if only three months a year, we understand the force that beckons from Mexico.

Each year, when Mister Will and I return to our home in Minnesota, we settle back in where we left off in our Midwest USA way of life...and we are content again. The stretching of our cultural bounds leaves us exhausted but exhilarated. We see home in a new light...fresh. But as the season stretches into late summer and early fall, we begin to hear again the metronome of a Latino beat, and our thoughts turn to Mexico.

Chapter 11 – There and Back...By Car

Lesson: Know How Fast You Want to Get There

It's all about the car. Mister Will loves his car. For more than a dozen years after purchasing Casa 4, we made the 2,300 mile drive one way, back and forth—a hefty 60,000 miles by my calculation. And all on the same roads.

You too might have the same inclination if your stay is several weeks or months and you like the idea of an exciting road trip. Folks who take to the long drive aren't all necessarily owners of Mexican property who one could reason might have more need for a car, as in ease of getting around for home maintenance, etc. We know renters who drive too. The difference seems more to be just in travel preferences: Those who choose to indulge in a few days on the road...kick back, nice and easy with all those motel stops, and those who prefer to get there fast. And, let's not forget that car-love I mentioned.

Mister Will and I eventually came up with another travel arrangement which, by the way, still includes a car, but I nevertheless want to share with you in this chapter our lessons learned in all those miles. You might be like us in favoring a good road trip. "Why not?" you might say. "Just jump in the car and go…no hassle with airports…just us and road." Yes, but slow down--first some tips and considerations. For the two of us, knowing what we know now, the 2,300-mile drive to Manzanillo, even with with all the hazards and unknowns, is still never totally out of the question…we might just jump in the car and go.

The Haul
So, you say, "Really...why drive?" What about wear and tear on the car...and you? What about the road hazards of long-distance driving? What about the big concerns of actually crossing that dangerous border by land? What about the logistics of travel in a foreign country?

Granted, for that first trip we needed to haul stuff; that was our rationale. How else were we to set up house, as it were, without our stuff, our car, our independence in getting around. Then, after that initiation, the next several drives seemed necessary too in furnishing and decorating our modest Casa 4. How convenient and economical, even how fun to haul whatever we could or might use in our winter escape.

Our small-sized SUV has been heaped with lamps and chairs, linens, curtains, bedspreads, dishes, a bread machine, an electric griddle, cookware of all sizes, a patio bench, a hand-crafted coffee table, shelving, power tools, air conditioners, fans, and even a kitchen stove. Whatever we couldn't find at the local Mexican stores was added each year to our "Bring to Mexico" list. In our basement back home, a special table was designated the drop-spot for items to haul on our next trip. We called it "the Mexico table." Most years the items spilled off to the floor space. And interestingly, the amount we accumulated always, *always,* fit in our car, as if we were wired to accumulate, accumulate...until a certain day we knew it was a good snug fit...and we stopped. Never did we resort to the unseemly, by our standards, hitching stuff up on the car rack.

So there is the hauling factor, legitimate for anyone setting up house in Mexico, I say. After all, every day, sensible travelers do haul stuff just to be practical, and that reasoning is how we have justified the danger. Shopping for any one of these particular items in Manzanillo, even now with updated shopping, can be a lengthy, frustrating, exhausting process and with less than satisfactory results. Even so, we necessarily end up shopping there in the Manzanillo area for what we ultimately learn are items not common in Mexico. And make do.

Included in the haul every year have been boxes of food stuffs, the likes of which might suggest a fear of eating anything too foreign for too long a time. Apparently three months is overly long to be without my self-designed low fat, low cholesterol, whole grain foods here at home from our high-priced, urban whole-food stores. As if Mexico, so rich with bounties of fresh fruits and vegetables, seafood and poultry, local cheeses, beans and nuts, baked-daily bagettes and, of course, fresh-grilled *tortillas,* can't satisfy, I have needed backup. For years on these trips, our car has been loaded with a three-month supply of items not easily found in Mexico: my precious whole wheat flour, unrefined white flour, corn meal (odd that the land of corn tortillas does not have corn meal), powdered skim milk, natural peanut butter, natural maple syrup, canned salmon, sweet pickle relish, Worcestershire sauce, chocolate chips, and Dove dark chocolates. Then for good measure I have tossed in extra oils and herbs from our Minnesota cupboards, just for start-up, I justified. This is a good argument to drive. Just throw in whatever fits.

After nearly ten years of this mentality, I finally saw the light: Stop the nonsense of hauling food when the choices available can be even better and certainly cheaper. What says full cultural emersion more than total reliance on the foods at hand? Just down the street can be found plentiful fruits and vegetables, fresh from the local farmers, and corn tortillas—the sacrosanct food in every Mexican home—are fresh and available warm even at convenience gas stops. A side benefit on this total reliance, of course, is the creative challenge posed, as in modifying recipes and substituting, say, pickled *chiles* for pickle relish in a tuna salad, or local cinnamon-infused chocolate chunks for Nestle chocolate chips in cookies. Certainly any cook worth her or his weight in corn *tortillas* should appreciate the simple but exotic nature of an unadulterated Mexican kitchen. *Buen provecho!*

So the food factor in hauling was finally alleviated. But even so, a few basic tricks have been helpful in order to successfully complete the trip with all of those other necessities we started with...you know, the furniture, appliance, those items. Here again, the risk is always lurking: might the border agents confiscate some belongings? You see the dark theme. But here we go with the tricks we've found most useful:

Our first year, a helpful expat advised us that the car should be "messy" at the border, so as not to bring attention, for instance, to new goods that we might be bringing into the country. No problem, I thought, considering the two full days of driving even before reaching the border; our car naturally looks messy by then. But more than that, she told us that any new items, appliances for instance, should be removed from their packaging.

Of course, that in effect camouflages the new items to look ordinary, and as a nice feature, adds more packing space. The "messiness" of a car jammed full, of course, lessens any desire an agent might have to inspect. We have encountered many a sleepy agent who waves us on after opening the car's back door to a wall of stuff.

That said, we have had to explain a couple of unusual items: The stove I mentioned did raise an eyebrow, laid there on its side so as to fit. "*Estufa*," I explained as the agent looked under the blanket and obviously could see it was a stove. I added, "*para mi cocina en Manzanillo...*" to explain that it was for my kitchen, not a charity. We hear that Mexico does not hanker to *Americanos* bringing items to the poor. The agent, still skeptical, then opened the oven door...I don't know, was he looking for drugs? Guns? A faint smile showed up in his eyes when he saw our stash of...books! Creative packing on the part of Mister Will, I thought.

Another suspicious item was a box of school supplies and backpacks we were delivering to a village on our route. The problem? The box, which happened to be just about the right size and shape for, say, rifles. Yes, several M15s might have fit quite nicely. There at the very back, we innocently and intentionally placed the box to be handy when we stopped at the village. Easy to reach, we reasoned, among all of our other items. And there at the very back, the box was prominent when the agent lifted the door. With a stern face, the agent pointed to it, meaning of course, "There, that box...open it!" We hurriedly explained in our limited Spanish something to the effect "things for school...for our friends." Not buying the explanation, the agent brought out her pocket knife and cut the tape. There in the box, of course, were the backpacks, each containing some basic school supplies. Again, a wry smile, and we were allowed to proceed. Since that trip, we carefully eyed our boxes as we packed.

Border Adventure

After given the go ahead by border agents and free to enter Mexico, Mister Will and I celebrated with open windows and flying hair as we barreled down the road. "Yipee!" Each and every pass at the border was a liberating experience. And in that first mile south of the border, as if to confirm that, yes indeed, we were in this new foreign land, far, far away, our cell phone coverage stopped, as if we had passed a wall barring cell phones—our connection gone. Catching on to this reality, we learned to make our calls to family just as we pulled out of the border crossing property. "Hey, it's us...just crossed the border...our cell phone will soon be out of service...no worries...will get back to you in a couple of days when we reach our casa...love you....[dead space]...hello, you still there...? [dead space]"

No matter that we were off the grid, now with miles adding between us and the border, the heavy cloud of anxiety evaporated and we were lightened as if on pure oxygen. The snacks came out, with radio tuned to foot-stomping country, we shed our jackets. The surrounding sage brush geography gave way to mountains in the distance. In two short hours we were high in the Sierra Madres, Clint Eastwood-type western backdrops, and like rough riders, we felt the rugged country...Mexico.

But let's back up a minute...the *entire* 2,300 miles is adventure, to be clear. The sheer tally of miles crossing varied landscapes and latitudes is exhilarating in itself. Road trip to Mexico! Never fail, the distinction of driving rather than flying draws gasps from many who are curious about distant Mexico. "Really? You don't say... How many miles is that anyway?" We tell them, and they gasp again. That then has been a segue into our escapades. We pause a second for full effect and then add as much or little as anyone wants to hear. I assume we have needed that attention.

But attention alone doesn't cut it when the reality is staring down the highway for ten hours a day, four days straight. The mind and the rear-end grow numb. And danger? Plenty of that, whether slick roads from ice or rain, poor visibility, heavy traffic, road construction, perilous navigation through cities, and speeding (or stand-still) semis—and that's all *before* even reaching the Mexican border. Once into Mexico, just double-down on these dangers and add in mountain roads, slow-moving rural pickups, speeding-bullet, high-end SUVs, sudden maneuvers for road work, foreign signage, immense cities, and occasional loose grazing livestock at the side of the road, all encountered even on Mexico's toll roads, and with a hefty fee. We stay alert.

Then, the danger that weighs heavily as we log the miles...the *madre* of all concerns that first comes to mind when considering a road trip to Mexico, the danger that puts Mexico on the black list for most vacationers traveling by car, the danger that movies are made of: the border. Whether it's an official warning from the State Department, alarming reports in the media, or hearsay concerns from well-meaning friends and relatives, we *do* acknowledge the risk. The border is that particularly hazardous place on the map where any drug traffic meets narco patrols head-on, and we as every day US citizens on our happy road trip are suddenly in that mix. Needless to say, the contraband has been en route across Mexico from God knows where for God knows how long without notice or concern by travelers on the same route, just whistling by. Who knows what is concealed in those semis or who is commanding that sleek SUV with the shaded windows? But it's there at the border, that very thin line between countries, when Mister Will and I automatically perked up and began to eye the other vehicles. Literally. Waiting in line, engines running, we could not help but conjure up intriguing and scary stories.

So we don't deny that the risks are there. We get how family and friends might be concerned and, if in their shoes, we would be too. I confess: I did have a mini-meltdown each year as we packed our bags and the time drew near to leave—second-guessing and third-guessing our wisdom of road travel. Mister Will and I talked it through, then talked it through some more, then more, to ease my jitters. And privately I wondered, maybe this was it for us. I could see the headlines: "Missing couple from Minnesota, presumed to be in northern Mexico, area of Monterrey. Last communication to family was just south of the border when cell phone coverage stopped." After Mister Will and I touched on all the lurking dangers, we packed the car.

And on that day of departure each year, as we backed out of our driveway just before sunrise, I said a teary goodbye to our house and our cozy Minnesota life, as if leaving a dear friend: "Take care, sweet house. See you soon. Hugs." And as we shifted into drive, I followed up with some serious Lutheran prayers for safe travels. We sped off.

We follow the media enough to know that narco traffic is a reality at the border, and especially at our particular crossing point: Laredo, Texas. Not just media hype. It happens that Laredo is the direct drug route to "el norte" via Interstate 35, which coincidentally for us, continues all the way to our very own Minneapolis, Minnesota. Imagine: Taking this drive might be crossing paths with the drug lords as we stop for a coffee at the Kum & Go in Missouri.

That first year, as our car clicked off the miles closer and closer to the border, the trepidation that Mister Will and I felt in our guts was evident...we rehearsed the process as we knew it and considered obstacles. With Mister Will at the wheel, I read aloud our AAA border information as set out in the Texas Tour Book, and then reread it, I checked and rechecked the whereabouts of our passports among the many zippered pockets of our "important papers bag," as we called it, I culled out and verified the documents that would be requested for our auto registration, and we practiced our limited Spanish words, as in the all-important greetings and social graces. Twenty-six border crossings later, the trepidation remained the same, coming or going.

No two crossings were even similar. That first year we would have sworn to the Virgin of Guadalupe that we knew the process: frontward, backward, we knew what we were doing. We couldn't have imagined that after crossing the Laredo Bridge No. 2 into Mexico, something so basic as signage directing to the immigration offices would be mysteriously absent. None. *Nada.* "Where do we go next? ...I didn't see a sign, did you? ...Wait. Stop! We are in Mexico now, and our car needs to be registered! We need to turn around! Now!"

Crossing that very bold line, from one side of the river to the other side of the river, we were instantly immersed in old Mexico, complete with crowded narrow streets and taco stands. As sudden as the change in a movie scene. We pulled up to the curb to ask directions. A local teenage boy, I'll call him Clever Boy, convinced us he knew the way, and the next minute we were off again, this time with Clever Boy joining us in the front seat (remember, our Honda was crammed full). This might have been the beginning of a harrowing kidnap situation, you say—"missing Minnesota couple, known to be traveling south through Laredo, Texas." Yes, but at some point in world travels especially, I believe we simply need to trust the common good. Clever Boy knew he could earn a few pesos standing there on the street coming off the bridge waiting for US cars just as ours with bewildered *gringos*. He delivered us roundabout to the *Puerta de Imigracion,* tucked inconspicuously underneath Bridge No. 2. Never mind the crazy location, Mister Will and I were euphoric with relief, and Clever Boy earned some *pesos* for lunch.

After that initiation to the Laredo border crossing, which, by the way, is cemented in our memory bank, we learned about another option for crossing just up the river some twenty miles, a newer facility to alleviate some of the traffic crossing in Laredo. Known as the Colombia Border Crossing, the facility is on its own out there in Texas sage brush country. That fact in itself is likely why it's more attractive than busy, congested Laredo. Forever, it seems, Mister Will and I will flinch at the memory of our ordeal at Bridge No. 2 in Laredo. Yet even at the less-threatening Colombia Crossing, the process was never smooth or consistent. Laws change. Forms change. Crowds change. One spring on our way back north, we didn't consider the end of the Easter holiday when families were on their drive back to the States. For well over two hours while we waited in line on the bridge, Mexican vendors walked among the cars to sell water and snacks as we sweltered in the heat.

The Christmas and New Year's holidays pose the same crowd scenarios. However, we did learn firsthand, and without any particular smart planning on our part, that most certainly New Year's Day is the quietest day of the year at the Mexican border entry. When Mister Will and I walked into the first area for initial processing of our tourist visas, on that morning of New Year's Day, no one was present in the main building, not even other customers. We waited and shuffled to be heard. We rang the bell next to the little Christmas ornament on the counter and shuffled again. "*Hola...hola?*" I finally spoke up toward the door into another room with the smell of cooked food wafting out. An agent finally surfaced, bleary-eyed, eating a taco. "Well naturally!" we reminded ourselves trying to hide our grins...at midmorning on New Year's Day who doesn't need more sleep?

Another miscue occurred when we took a new route home with a crossing at Nogales into Arizona. Friends familiar with the route instructed us on the details, except for this one crucial alert: The Mexican facility for processing an auto return is located twenty miles before the border, not *at* the border as we were accustomed in Texas, and *not* obvious to someone new on the road. Now, keep in mind, the exact location of the auto return is a very, very important detail because it is there that you receive your hefty $500 deposit back for returning with a US vehicle. No return of the vehicle, no money back. Mister Will and I whistled on into Nogales only to suddenly find ourselves welcomed by the US border agents. Wait! The USA flag! First should have been a Mexican facility! Mister Will shouted out the window in a downpour, "Where did we go wrong, sir? We need to return our vehicle registration. Please!" The US agent, unmoved, gestured a u-turn to go back on the road we had just traveled. "Really? You have to be kidding, sir? No? [chuckle]" Mister Will tried his darnest to humor the agent, as though we could be given a pass. But no, we turned around. Twenty miles back into Mexico and in the downpour we did eventually find the tiny booth, hidden again it seemed. There we completed the paperwork for our Toyota.

On Mexican Roads

Driving in Mexico is its own adventure. Do proceed with extra caution as advised: DO NOT leave the car unattended (as at a gas station where gangs might plant drugs in your car), DO NOT drive on backroads (as in less-traveled areas where gangs or just ordinary banditos might be encountered), DO NOT drive too fast or too slow (as to call attention from the *federales* who might hijack your cash), and, by all means, DO NOT have an accident (as in all bets are off for a fair trial). These are standard, common-sense guidelines when traveling in Mexico—several notches up, wouldn't you say, from our biggest travel advice back home: DO buckle your seat belt (which, by the way, is often ignored in Mexico). Just the *possibility* of ending up in a Mexican jail is enough to stay at full attention.

Then too, common sense rules apply for general safety when traveling: DO park at night in a secured area, and at all times DO keep an eye on the surroundings. These basic rules became second nature for us, like automatically shifting into another gear the moment we crossed the Rio Grande: "Okay, now we're *here*...new rules." This is what our hard-wired memory tells us. Then, all of Mexico was there for us to enjoy in a more relaxed mode.

But really, go through with all this? What every day, sensible traveler would choose an itinerary with all of the above-mentioned threats? Is it a subversive lust for the dangerous unknown? Or for breaking all the rules? What is it about cross-country Mexico?

Now a word or two about toll roads: First learning about the extensive miles of toll roads that crisscross Mexico and then adding up the cost, we wondered, "Is it really worth it? Why not take our time and save a few pesos by staying on the roads marked *libre,* free?" The answer: Absolutely with emphasis, use the toll roads! Not only are the toll roads wider, smoother and usually four-lane, they also are free from much of the local truck traffic, which especially gums up the traffic flow through mountainous passes. And, as a good backup, the toll roads offer up assistance by the Green Angels, a government-paid, bilingual crew that patrol the toll roads throughout Mexico—easy to identify in their green trucks. Just call 078. The Green Angels are available twenty-four hours a day by phone but may not be available for roadside assistance in the evening; after all, the golden rule is to avoid driving in Mexico after nightfall. Mister Will and I do not have a personal story about the Green Angels, except to say that we are comforted to know they are just a phone call away.

Our tallied cost in US dollars for tolls from Laredo to our Manzanillo has run about $150.00. Not cheap. But Mister Will and I learned after a wrong step onto a *libre* route around the monster of a city San Luis Potosi, that paying whatever amount is worth it. We were held up an extra two hours that day.

Up until recently, Pemex has been the gasoline monopoly in Mexico. Now, in our city of Manzanillo, we know of a Shell station too, and we hear about other gas companies showing up, likely in the large cities. But for us, through all the many years of driving cross country in Mexico, it's been Pemex we still keep an eye out for. So that is how I will frame this advice.

After leaving the US at Laredo, Texas, and heading south, it's no more BP, Holiday, Cenex, Standard, or the unnamed little pump on the corner; it's the big green and white Pemex sign you're looking for. Some say a Pemex can be found every sixty miles or so on the toll roads, so no worries when the tank is low. I for one like to have a lot more than sixty miles left in the tank when venturing through Mexico. Who needs the worry of being stranded on the high plains of Mexico? Always intriguing too are the Pemex stations that aren't functioning: seemingly brand-new facilities appear unfinished or abandoned with boarded-up doors and weeds sprouting through cracks in the concrete, as though someone in the Pemex oil family made a poor choice with that location or that funding mysteriously ceased. So banking on a Pemex in the next sixty miles seems overly risky when the tank is low or when someone in the car particularly needs a restroom stop. Plan ahead.

Much like the availability of gasoline in Mexico, the availability of basic, secure lodging for a Mexican road trip can be sketchy. Unlike travels at home where a Holiday Inn or Motel 6 is just up the road, in Mexico the distance between options for an acceptable overnight room can be another two hundred miles. Again, plan ahead.

Each year when Mister Will and I left the border crossing at Colombia at about noon on a given day, we knew that we had two acceptable options for a motel that night in the deep interior of Mexico: either six hours away in Matehuala or eight hours away in San Luis Potosi. That two hours of wiggle room allowed for any unforeseen circumstance that might delay our travel into the dark hours after sunset, which in all these years we have been dutifully instructed by travel guides and the US State Department, no less, as a definite no-no. Do not drive after dark. The villages in between offer up only a string of minimal but colorful concrete-block cafés along the roadway: "Cafe de Rosa," "Cafe de Lolita," "Cafe de Maria," and occasional roadhouses that appear isolated and highly questionable for a host of other reasons: "Ranchero Esquisito," "Fiesta La Luna," "Hotel de Vaqueros."

Another telling feature of this remote stretch of highway is the harsh landscape. Sagebrush and Joshua trees stretch for miles butting up to the Sierra Madres off in the distance on both sides of the highway, and winds whip up dust swirls rising twenty, thirty feet from the ground. Except for the few sparse villages along the highway, the land appears void of people. The arresting landscape mesmerizes. But as we hurry along on our toll road, eventually it's a vendor we see at the side of the road, then another and another, waving from their makeshift lean-tos. Their wares we make out are snake skins and vessels of snake oils hanging from limbs of brush. Waving would seem a futile effort in coaxing any car to stop amidst traffic speeding by at 120km, but these desperate people flail their arms like cries for help. The only protection these wanting souls have from the unrelenting sun and wind-blown sand are ragged tarps of plastic or cloth affixed to a fence post or an outcropping of scrub brush. Who, I wonder, are the customers? Never have we witnessed any. But one year we did stop, and I knew as I got our of the car that it was a mistake. The weather-beaten slip of a woman with pleading empty eyes grabbed my arm to show me her snake skins, the oils, the nibs of cactus in tiny pots at her feet. And then she pointed to my shirt and sandals and gestured for a possible trade: my clothing for anything she was selling. I regret to say this was not my finest moment: I hurried back to the safety of the car. I grabbed one of those tiny cacti on the way, shoved pesos into her palm, and waved a goodbye from the closed window. I don't recall any change in her hollow expression as we sped away.

But second chances do come around, they say. After our experience with the "snake people," as we now refer to that stop, Mister Will and I each year planned a drop-off of school supplies at any one of the villages we passed on our drive, like an impromptu, anonymous gift. We certainly do not take credit for the idea; this really swell concept in charity we learned from our dear Wisconsin friends who over their forty years driving to Mexico have handed out not only school supplies and backpacks, but clothing, shoes, toys, candy, and whatever else fit in their truck. The item they are most proud to donate are wheelchairs—that's right, wheelchairs—that they manage to collect during the year back home in Wisconsin. This unwieldy load each year is packed tightly along with their own gear into their Chevy Tahoe, and yes, at the border they do need to be on their toes with this unusual big haul. After passing inspection, they have their goods to give away at will as they head south through Mexico. Their advice to us has been simply this: Do not veer off the main road more than, say, a quarter mile, as in why flirt with danger. Gringos do not need to draw further attention by meandering in the back roads far from assistance. And, do pack the give-away items at the back door of the vehicle for easy access—be organized. Any personal items spilling out in all the chaos of the distribution might get left behind. Recall how we positioned that odd-shaped box filled with backpacks at the rear—the box that raised an alert with the border patrol.

Emboldened by these spirited friends, Mister Will and I took the challenge. Our efforts were very scaled-down versions in comparison, minimal really—our couple of boxes fitting into our Toyota versus our friends' trailer bed worth of stuff in their Tahoe. But the concept was still there. With the help of our family in Minnesota, Mister Will and I focused on collecting school bags and supplies each December before heading south. The drop-off wasn't quite as easy as we supposed. First, selecting the village depended on the location of a school or park visible from the highway, and whether the village in fact had a school or a park, plus of course spotting some children. An on-the-spot decision was our default method of selection; that is, after a quick ninety-degree scan as we slowed through the city limits. "There!" I blurted that first year as I pointed to a tiny church along the service road. "Looks like a couple of kids with adults working around that little church...let's give it a go....here, turn here!" Mister Will by now had passed the turn, so he doubled-back at the next *retorno*. Once off the highway, we were on a rough, dirt road, a path really, which brought us to the group outside the church. I searched for my Spanish words to locate a possible school. *"Donde esta la escuela?"* They all turned to point farther down the gnarly, rutted road. "*Gracias!*" Mister Will and I waved and bounced along another few hundred feet toward an assortment of concrete buildings, although nothing even remotely looked like a school. We asked more passersby. Yes, we were going in the correct direction. "*Derecho*," they said, again pointing farther down the way. Finally, at the trail's end, literally, we stopped abruptly in front of a longer block building. "Yes, that must be the school, with the row of bright green windows...see?" By now, the townspeople were assembling to witness this odd sight of gringos older than average driving a US Toyota Highlander through their community on a roadway more suitable for scooters or burros.

A bit clunky in execution, this was our endeavor for charity. In the end, we accomplished our goal: supplies were delivered, and we had the satisfaction of stretching our cultural bounds. But our donation in fact was complicated because of the Christmas-New Year holiday, which in Mexico extends well into January and coincides with our trip south. That's the window of time every year when Mister Will and I happened to be in this remote spot in the middle of Mexico. The holiday meant the school was closed and the teacher was at her home in a nearby village. So as the townspeople stared with quizzical eyes, Mister Will and I hopped to work coordinating an on-the-spot distribution of backpacks to the children based on school age, and we handed over miscellaneous supplies to one of the women for eventual delivery to the teacher. Our strung-together Spanish words seemed to convey the idea. But so quickly our gifts were gone—how we wished for more to give! We could have done much better, this we agreed as we turned back onto our highway. The nagging question was this: Which children were left without?

We did stop again the next year, and this time the residents in fact recognized our Toyota as we turned onto their rutted road, as if they had been waiting for us, their holiday guests. All smiles, they hurried to gather in front of the school just as the previous year. This time our gifts included a more expansive array of supplies, plus other incidentals and candy. Still, in our minds, the handout was not enough. Efforts to communicate with the teacher during the year had been fruitless, but what were we to expect with an email address, half legible, likely misunderstood. Our broken Spanish was acceptable, but no doubt we cast the usual gringo barrier in our hurry to keep on schedule. I'm quite positive I peeked at my watch during this gathering, to consider the many miles ahead of us for our intended destination that day before sundown.

The more in-depth conversation which we *should* have had would have explained our frustration and would have asked the specific needs for another year. "What would be especially helpful for your school?" we should have asked. We could have talked about *our* families—our kids and grandchildren—who contributed so generously, and we could have learned something more about *their* families. Learned some names, really become connected. And, we could have asked, "How, might we do this more equitably?"

Here is where a charitable organization makes perfect sense: Write a check to say, United Way, and let someone else figure out the dynamics of who gets what. The built-in 15% administration is well worth it, now we know. And for the love of fairness, in this manner we can avoid the awkward face-to-face circumstance, especially involving another culture and language. Just forget about the big excited eyes of those children. These thoughts Mister Will and I shared as we left the village that second time. But the lovely people of *Comunidad de los Minas,* however, had other thoughts on their minds. As we drove away, they applauded...like a grace note.

We haven't returned to that village along the highway. Circumstances involving a late schedule that next year plus major road construction at that particular turnoff, forced us to press on down the road that day. Our handout packages were still with us when we arrived in Manzanillo. So, our second-best option was to deliver the supplies to a school in a neighboring community with our Manzanillo. We agreed on this more organized approach from then on. We waited for the schools to open again after the holidays to have the attention of a teacher—still face-to-face, two cultures, two languages, but with oversight and knowledge in an appropriate use of the supplies. But each year at that time over the holidays I continue to wonder if our friends in *Comunidad de los Minas,* still wait for our Toyota.

In Mexican Hotels

Accommodations en route through the middle of Mexico are another topic worthy of discussion. If you find yourself on a road trip through Mexico, take note that AAA-worthy motels are few and far between; Mexico is a big country with vast open spaces between large cities. The reputable and quite comfortable motels/hotels that Mister Will and I settled on years ago on our southwest route from Loredo, whether our stop for the night was in Matehuala or in San Luis Potosi, remained as beacons in a wasteland as we added on the miles into deep Mexico. A good night's rest awaited us. The decision between one or the other city was based on how many miles we had before sunset. We usually were conservative.

But one January when we were delayed more than usual at the border and therefore behind schedule, we defied the common-sense rules above mentioned and drove the extra two hours, now late afternoon. The sun soon settled behind the mountains, and our daytime-friendly highway now was a danger in the dark.

Fast-moving and slow-moving traffic were hazards: the sleek SUVs speeding to Mexico City, the lumbering tour buses, and the miniature farm pickups with swaying loads of produce stacked precariously high. Those desolate villages, I mentioned, held jolting and heart-stopping surprises with unmarked speed *topes,* pedestrians popping out of the ditches, and farm animals feeding in the median. Mister Will slowed down. Even the city lights as we finally entered San Luis Potosi seemed distractions as we muscled our way through dense traffic and wrong turns to eventually stop at our hotel. Weary beyond words and grateful for our safe delivery, Mister Will and I toasted to "Day 3," knowing full well the risks of those extra miles closer to our destination.

A very special and unique type of motel accommodation is common in Mexico, though Mister Will and I had yet to learn this as we made that first trip. The "no-tell motel," we came to find out, has quite the following among many of our Canadian and US friends who, like us, drive to and from Mexico. "Sure!" they exclaim with wide smiles and a wink when asked if they know about these places. "We've stayed at one or two of them. They're cheap, secure...and very clean!"

Apparently, the question of *"not* very clean" was what was on my mind that night after Mister Will and I pulled into the unusual place situated just on the outskirts of Guadalajara. We had been lost for hours in the sprawling city of six million people. Detour after detour had distorted our sense of direction, and this frustrating, exhausting scenario was what we were facing after a full ten hours on narrow, perilous mountainous roads. Miraculously, just at that precise moment when I knew without a doubt that driver Mister Will was nearing the end of his classic indomitable patience, a well-placed roundabout spun us out onto the exact tollway we needed to continue on toward Manzanillo. "Wow! It's a miracle!"

But night was closing in; remember, no driving after dark. With the toll booth just ahead, as well as unknown and possibly perilous territory into the thick of night, Mister Will swerved into a last-minute driveway posting a motel sign with something like "*El Delfin.*" First clue of something slightly off-kilter: down the long landscaped driveway we encountered the likes of a ticket booth with dark shaded glass. Like ordering up a burger at a drive-through, Will asked into the microphone, "Do you have a room tonight for two?" He held up two fingers.

I spoke up across the seat, *"cama matrimonio,"* meaning double bed which I was so proud to communicate just off the top of my head after this long day.

"*Si, si,*" from behind the dark glass. And the gate swung open. We proceeded ahead as directed.

Second clue: A hotel employee dressed in crisp housekeeping attire met us near a line of garages and directed us like a traffic cop into one with the door raising. Just as our rear bumper barely cleared the garage entrance, the door was already on its way down. There we sat in the dark, closed garage somewhere in the middle of Mexico.

Third clue: The ingratiating señora, speaking in *muy rapido* Spanish, walked us through the garage door *directly* into the one-bedroom unit. There, in the style of Wheel of Fortune, she proceeded to show off the humongous round bed, the mirrored ceiling, the mammoth screen television with giant speakers, the glassed-in shower with sunken hot tub, and the artwork on the walls, stylishly erotic. The chest of drawers, Mister Will later pointed out, was fake furniture painted on the wall.

By now, I was getting the picture. In my exhausted state of mind, hysteria was soon to follow in now this impending decision facing us—well, me—of where to stay that night. Nowhere in my sensible, good-girl past had I been confronted with this scenario. In contrast, Mister Will, without a bit of concern, had already seated himself on the bed—no chairs in this setup—and, I swear to the Patron of Travelers, was ready to take off his shoes and lie down, exhausted as he was.

"*Ventanas?*" I blurted as I searched the walls for any sign of a window, which in my mind might qualify the place as somewhat normal. The room was basically a bed in a cave. "*No ventanas?*" Even I surprised myself at this outburst and quick word choice in Spanish. I knew I had hit on something with the sudden quizzical look of the señora—no way had windows ever been an issue in this place. I repeated, now with conviction and in a slightly accusatory tone with my arms tightly crossed, "*No ventanas?*" Now in my hyper state, that's all the Spanish I could muster.

But to my dismay, we weren't out of there yet. Señora's eyes narrowed as she thought of options. Then with a smile, "*Uno momento, por favor, mi amigos...*" We were gestured to follow. Out of that garage and into another, same deal. Down the long row of units, we entered a similar space, but it was the bathroom that was the focus this go-round. With a grand flourish, she gestured to the wall next to the hot tub: "*Ventana!*" Mister Will and I bent down to look, as this window was very low, likely just the proper height if, say, relaxing in the spacious tub, and it was just a smite larger than a mail dropbox. Apparently what we saw through this slice of window was a lovely courtyard. By now Mister Will had the picture too, but his included a distraught wife incapable even to sit in these quarters, not to mention get a decent night's sleep.

That night in January 2005, as we turned out of the driveway from *El Delfin* and back on to the toll road headed out of town, now with stars out and a big Mexico moon. I reached in our bag of snacks for a couple of Snickers and I emptied the thermos into our coffee mug. "Maybe this will help," I managed. Mister Will settled back in his seat, turned on the radio to a Mexican ballad, and rested his hand on mine as he picked up speed. "Colima should be only a couple hours away. Maybe we'll find a place in Colima."

Finding the Way

One would think that the utter chaos we experienced in that first visit to Guadalajara—never mind the no-tell motel scenario—would sink in and clarify any route discrepancies through that city another time. We should have learned something, right? Well no...it's a fact that the next twenty-five passes through over the years would be fraught with missed turns. Even now as we take road trips in Mexico, the big cities challenge us. If not for detours around construction, it's the signage that seems to get us. We might be watching ever so diligently for a sign with the name "Lazaros" when the sign we inevitably miss perhaps abbreviates to "Laz" and only at the end, as in "Av. de Rob. Laz." As we are speeding by at 60 miles per hour in the six lanes of traffic, I might catch Laz but then it's too late. Baffled, an hour later we find our way again. Or, we misinterpret a sign for the main highway and careen off, only to wind up on a narrow street lined with taco stands and loud music, or even more interesting, a narrow street lined with vendors displaying toilets...lots of toilets.

Even our GPS can't be trusted: Lost in translation, the technology misses subtle road deviations in Mexico. After years of attempts to navigate the city GPS style, we came to understand that the GPS has some language problems too. GPS doesn't recognize the particular Mexican turnoffs which are standard in large Mexican cities; the turnoffs happen, as we have since learned, not at the turnoff but just before the intended intersection. And the intended intersection offers no access. You see how we could go wrong. Guadalajara, the sprawling mega city and the last of our traffic hurdles on our 2,300-mile route, the city which certainly must boast the most lost foreigners, that unforgiving city that Mister Will and I needed to deftly circumnavigate on our route to and from Manzanillo—that city of Guadalajara soon earned the code name "Evil City."

The unfolding high drama as we traveled by car back and forth had for us an addicting edge. Apparently so, since that was our choice for so many years. Even now, we grow nostalgic when remembering those miles, every one of them. The worn highway map with our route highlighted in bright yellow holds the stories we cherish. As much as we complained and moaned each year when we finally arrived either in Mexico or back home, totally spent, when it was that day on the calendar for us to leave again, we were eager to go. This might be you with a love for road trips.

In Mexico, it's likely the bragging rights we share with other North American road travelers there that translate to entertainment as we compare routes, roadside accommodations, near misses, and border incidences, amidst laughs about getting lost. All this over drinks. "The Evil City" raises a toast every time. As it happens, everyone we know who has driven the route has the same knee-jerk reaction at the mention of the city. Here back in Minnesota, it's that adventure factor I mentioned, which Mister Will and I hold fast between us—a bit of rebellion, I am guessing, in going against the norm for persons like us of this certain age, and that is what we see in our friends who drive. We will tackle Guadalajara any day of the week if that's what it takes to get to our Manzanillo destination.

Another Option...or Not

Is there another way? Well, yes, of course! Air travel is the accepted mode for almost all of our friends and acquaintances who winter in Mexico. Even with poor airline connections, including an overnight, the trip is quick and efficient compared to our long days on the road. And costs are comparable. Yet, Mister Will and I have been enamored by the whimsical notion of taking off in our car on any given winter day, packed for adventure with the car pointed south. No worries about a flight to catch. And in the spring, when Mexico breezes are hot and humid and our thoughts turn to tulips blooming in Minnesota, we have eagerly awaited the day for taking off again, car pointed north. No worries about a flight to catch. We seemed to experience a road trip high. Even now with our new plan of travel, we sometimes long for the feel of the road again. To us, a flight is just a mode of transportation while a road trip is, well, a trip.

There is another plus in driving worth mentioning, and this is no small factor: Once there, you have a car. Wheels. Whether the destination is the supermarket, church, hardware store, distant beach, restaurant, airport, or a city in unknown parts of Mexico, we relied on our Toyota to get us there. Buses and taxis have their rightful purpose, but owners of property in Mexico really do need a car – that's our advice. In fact, most of the people we know who own a condo in Mexico, also have a car in Mexico. Mister Will and I have done our share of busing and taxiing throughout Mexico and found both modes perfectly useful and cheap, and we are grateful for those options. In fact, for city-to-city travel, Mexico has an incredible network of buses that crisscross the country. A ten-hour bus ride through the mountains is not unusual for the locals traveling to see family.

But relying on taxis or city buses for day-to-day travel needs severely restricts those activities. I'm thinking first about the numerous trips Mister Will and I make to the hardware stores for casa maintenance and then of course about the trips for groceries or trips for fun just because. Those trips for fun can add enormous scope to a cross-cultural vacation. Case in point: Our on-the-spot decision to attend a rodeo just north of town. "Hey, that sounds like fun...let's go!" We zoomed off in our Toyota as the sun was setting and made our way on small new roads, through a village, over a creek, and finally onto a lighted field with bleachers and 10-foot high speakers, dancing horses, cowboys, and vendors selling spicy treats from the grills and six-packs of cold *cervesas,* not single beers but six-packs. There we became enveloped with families of *Mexicanos,* just the two of us gringos smiling and laughing among all of them to the sounds of mariachi under the bright lights that night. That's what having a car can do for you.

Our friends who fly and do not have the use of a car woudn't have it any other way. No worries about parking, insurance, traffic, road hazards, or carting folks around. They get where they want to go, which is usually by bus, and they understand the limitations of routes and schedules. And, to their credit, they are tireless walkers, all in fine physical shape. Off and on over the years I have even wished for that kind of freedom without a car. I find the greener option of travel very attractive and smart. But Mister Will sees nothing attractive or smart about hoofing in the hot sun to catch a bus, especially when the bus route doesn't quite get to the destination in mind, thus requiring more hoofing in the hot sun. He's not even accepting of the use of taxis except in unusual circumstances. In other words, the car makes life much easier and more comfortable.

So, for us, the car has been a given, and that adds up to 14-some years commuting to Mexico. At some point, a wise person might point out, we are too damned old for this. Buy a ticket and fly! Use the bus! Use a taxi! But wait, we were on to yet another idea: What if we had access to a car while in Manzanillo? In that case, Mister Will and I could fly to Mexico and then get around by car as accustomed. First thought would be to rent a car, but renting for a three-month stay can be a costly nightmare. So that was out. But owning a vehicle outright, which then could be stored those months when back home, well, that would be a win-win. Fly and drive.

Storage of a car in Mexico has been yet another obstacle, especially when deciding whom to trust with that storage. Stories have circulated among those of us with like minds about having a Mexican car, that gringo-cars in long-term storage are fair game. Is the odometer a reliable gage, we wonder. Something might be slightly amiss about the car when the owner returns, so the puzzle sounds something like this: Hmm…someone was driving our car while we were gone for nine months, but who...and where...and holy *chihuahua!* What happens next?

But first things first, we decided: get the damned car. That was our mission. Odds are that we would find reputable storage in due time after we had talked to enough people. The problem was that we as foreigners simply did not know/did not understand how to get this done...this mystery of owning a Mexican car. Are we "tourists," as labeled on our visas, allowed to own a Mexican car? Or, do we need to be "temporary residents?" Just what *is* the process and paperwork required to own a vehicle in Mexico? Answers to these and a dozen or more other questions, no one seemed to know. The snag of government regulations and restrictions continues to dull the senses.

When bureaucratic hurdles get in the way of foreigners wishing to invest even *more* into Mexico, such as a car for example, then foreigners tend to come up with ideas of their own. Mister Will and I personally have knowledge of autos brought into Mexico, and those autos intentionally have *stayed* in Mexico. This approach relies on the notion that Mexico's system of tracking foreign vehicles is slow and antiquated. The sneaky idea is to legitimately cross the border with the proper papers and pay the fee, but then fly home and keep the vehicle in Mexico. Just stay one step ahead of the border agents. Who's the wiser? In fact, even an outdated US license plate usually goes unnoticed tooling around the country of Mexico; this we have learned firsthand from friends. Recall our seller's unfortunate incident with the car bomb landing in her Dodge? Well, that Dodge was still drivable so she gave it to Roque who then drove it another five years, all the while still with the outdated Minnesota plates.

The thought is that ideally the car that is intended to remain in Mexico without detection should be an older model. Older models don't get much attention, and if the authorities catch on and confiscate it, well, the car wasn't worth that much to begin with. When Mister Will and I have crossed into Mexico each year by car, our vehicle registration has allowed us four months before returning the Toyota to the border. When we have crossed back into the States from Mexico, our vehicle registration fee is returned. So you see, that's where someone might think it a clever idea to hang onto the car, store it, and make future trips by air. All that is lost would be the vehicle registration fee that was collected upon entry—comparatively a small price for the use of a car. Who knows if and when the border data is tracked, but we do know that some do take the risk of driving an unauthorized foreign vehicle.

Mister Will and I have not been alone in this predicament of sketchy information in regards to owning a Mexican vehicle. Among our friends who drive to Mexico, this complex topic of vehicle ownership with the accompanying issue of storage in

Mexico, or just plain driving in Mexico, is routine conversation. It goes like this: Why *not* circumvent the law? After all, none of us can get answers. All we're trying to do is drive here in this country that, oh by the way one can wager, is boosted mightily by the pesos we spend. But here again to be fair, in the US many undocumented Mexicans face similar hurdles to drive legally, all the while supporting our economy.

The story we return to time and time again for this rationale of circumventing the law is about an acquaintance—a foreigner like us—who though legally blind somehow obtained a Mexican driver's license...yes, legally blind. Using that example as a starting point, we have speculated: Just maybe, the requirements at the border are a bit loose as well. Just maybe, we could drive our US car into Mexico and leave it to use indefinitely, license outdated, and no one the wiser. Or, just maybe, we ought to continue our pursuit of driving legally in Mexico. After all, foreigners, no matter where, need to be accountable. Nonetheless, back and forth, the debate.

Interesting to compare, however, is the strict enforcement of parking tickets in our Manzanillo. Recall the incident I noted in Chapter 10: X Cultures. The US certainly can learn a thing or two from the *departmento municipal* about collecting fines. When Mister Will and I were ticketed in downtown Manzanillo for parking ever-so-slightly over a crosswalk, we set the ticket aside and continued with our errands for that day. Of course, we intended to take care of the ticket soon, maybe the next day, the next week, whenever...but we knew that the effort would require another trip to downtown Manzanillo with a visit at the busy government building. That evening following the parking violation, as we stepped out to our car to meet friends for dinner, we noticed that our license plates were missing. "Of all the luck," I muttered and stomped, "first a parking violation and then someone steals our plates! Who would go to the trouble of removing our plates?" The answer, we were to learn, was the Manzanillo City Police. They had stealthily tracked us down that very day, removed the plates, and delivered them to an offsite facility where the plates were tucked in a massive file drawer for such matters to be held until payment. No note, no telephone call, *no comunicado*. Roque recognized the situation right away. "Mister Will, did you get a parking ticket?" With Roque alongside, Mister Will found the offsite facility, maneuvered the maze of tellers, paid the pesos (roughly a pittance, $7.00 US, and by the way, much less than Mister Will was willing to pay the officer), and returned with our Mexican plates. An afternoon's work.

So, to assume that Mexico's border patrol is lax or behind in its administrative duties is only short-sighted, hopeful thinking and not by any means a sure bet. Trouble might be waiting for you at the border the next time you cross. Among our compatriots on this car ownership issue, someone always was on to a new idea, yet no one came up with the go-to procedures or rules of Mexican vehicle ownership by a foreigner. Just one mere visit with an immigration agent usually squelched any enthusiasm for the subject...who knew that Spanish could be so difficult and rules so vague? "Do you have a pamphlet on the subject?" we inquired. "Something on the computer?" Just a shake of the head was all we could get from the stern agent behind the desk.

Word still is that those procedures and regulations vary with the change of Mexican government leaders so that oftentimes even the local auto salesmen are not clear on the details of ownership by foreigners. The quagmire of Mexican customs regulations always stops us short. "There's got to be a way," we all agree, and then we move on to another subject because we all assume that the answer is locked in the mystic of Mexico. We give up.

But as it happened, in our fourteenth year of this Mexican adventure, surprise, surprise, Mister Will and I solved the car issue, once and for all. Not a one-step process by any means. First, we endured multiple, mind-numbing visits to immigration offices, initially in our own St. Paul and then in our own Manzanillo, with the purpose of gaining a new status, "temporary resident." Seemingly endless forms, interviews in broken Spanish and English, multiple mugshots...stamp, stamp, stamp...this was our mission. The new status would allow us to own a Mexican car, so we understood, and then finally we could end the crazy long commutes back and forth to Minnesota. Flying would be the new us. And Mister Will, for his perseverance over the years, would still have his car.

Likely even a *Mexicano* will acknowledge that anything business or administrative or official or even clerical in Mexico is extraordinarily confusing, complicated, and tough to accomplish, a veritable maze of wrong turns with a marathon effort. Then factor in us foreigners attempting to accomplish the task. The car deal is such an example: No one has said for sure whether or not Mister Will and I actually needed that new status "temporary resident" to buy our car. The law changed, some say. But the CURP number assigned in that process did in fact aid when we sat down with the Nissan dealer to purchase our Versa. As it turns out, the CURP number remains with you forever, somewhat like our Social Security number in the US.

The temporary resident status, we would learn, in fact was not suited for us, spending only three or four months in Mexico. Unless planning to become a permanent resident or staying in the country for more than four months, the classification for us would be a waste of $600.00 per year, and let's not forget the pain and suffering in the immigration office for each renewal. Therefore, we terminated that status, and we each remain the common "tourist."

So, there you have it: We made the switch from driving to flying, and our little Nissan Versa is waiting for us when we arrive in Manzanillo. And like finding the last piece of a puzzle, the answer to winter storage was there all along: at the Nissan dealership. All in all, a humbling exercise.

Without a doubt, combining the air travel with an on-site car of our own is a win-win for efficiency and freedom. Our little 2014 Nissan sedan...with our very own cool Mexican license plate for the state of Colima...feels like it has been waiting for us *Americanos* all along. Even the extraordinarily good sound system for such a modest vehicle suggests a Mexican influence. After all, shouldn't the norm in all Mexican vehicles be quality speakers to bring out the rich base rhythms? Furthermore, now with our Mexican wheels, we experience an even broader awareness of the culture, for even if just labeled "tourists," we now know a little more about the day-to-day life in our Manzanillo. Insurance, storage, upkeep, the invaluable services of our trustworthy mechanic down the block ...these are the topics of car ownership here in Mexico. We are proud. So yes, I'm fond of our Nissan. If not for Mister Will's insistence and his dogged efforts, I'm afraid I too would be moaning a loss of car independence. Our independence. As it is, when and where we want to go, we go. And we go with Mexican plates.

Chapter 12 - The Ties That Bind

Lesson: Know Who and What You Are Leaving and for How Long

Choosing to be away from home for a chunk of the year should not be taken lightly; home is where the heart is, as the saying goes. Family is the main and first social group to consider when planning a time away from home. It's family that is foremost in the conversations among our friends while in Mexico; we visitors to Mexico are alike in that our families are far, far away. We share the concerns and relish in the joys of our particular families and are always alert to any kids, grandkids, brothers, or sisters who just might visit.

The emergency I mentioned in my introduction was in fact about family. So, I do know a thing or two about the sickening feeling of being far—too far—away from home for important family events, even to include, God forbid, an emergency. That was the lesson in store for us the winter of 2011 as we frantically rushed home to be with our son. That lesson was a wake-up call that not only confronted an increasing long-term worry but forced us into a better communication system in future Mexico trips. Our story did have a good ending. But the fear of leaving family responsibilities still leaves a mark. It's family that weighs heavily into the equation of pluses and minuses for a peaceful Mexico getaway.

Then the other social ties. "Reference group"—that's the term our sociology professor friend used when he first heard us talk about our friends back home in Minnesota—our group that evolved over four decades based on one interest: running. Those are the people we were leaving behind and who apparently were coming up often in our everyday talks with our new friend in Manzanillo—often enough that he told us about reference groups. In our excitement for Mexico, we neglected to think through our social ties at home.

The Minnesota group meets every Saturday morning, rain or shine, for a three- to ten-mile run at the city lakes, followed with breakfast: simple, casual, diverse, and not-to-be-missed. Even now, as our group has aged and the intensity of our workouts has lessened, we still focus any extra get-togethers around an outdoor physical activity, as in biking or hiking. And, over the years, the children from our group of friends have grown up with this inclination, even joining in with us now as young adults and some even with children of their own at our Saturday morning run. So we're intergenerational active sorts.

Why does this matter? Our professor friend explained in sociology terms that we "refer" to a group such as this in evaluating ourselves and in guiding our behavior and attitudes. A reference group might be card players, churchgoers, winter enthusiasts, gourmet foodies, bowlers, any number of sporting groups, and so on and so on. As for Mister Will and myself, exercise and outdoor activity have guided our choices throughout our lives. Whether running, biking, swimming, or hiking, we have centered ourselves with like-minded people. It's even how we chose each other, meeting that first time at an exercise class at the YMCA. The two of us have tallied up some forty-five marathons. And not only have we run marathons ourselves, we are spectators at marathons and other road races and track events, even watching such events on television. Statistics of track and field events hold our attention. We know specifications for running shoes, as in which shoe brand fits which body type, and we know all too well the difference between supination and pronation, which, if you are wondering, is basically foot plant, an indicator of future knee problems. These oddities are the topics of interest in our Minnesota running group. It's the curious nature of our social group that Mister Will and I have been leaving for three months each year—our dear reference group. No wonder they pop up in our conversations while away those three months every year.

Take note on what this means for you should you be inclined to leave home for a lengthy period. Who guides your behavior and attitudes? What part of your social structure are you leaving behind? And how long is too long to be away from that social group? Our move to Mexico meant a move away from our fitness tribe for three months each year.

You see now why the dirt track was such a big deal in our purchase decision. It made perfect sense for us. We saw the outdoor track as a nod from God that, yes, Casa 4 so close by was just the place for a slightly offbeat older couple like ourselves who happen to like to run outdoors. For you, the feature that tips the scales for your purchase or your long-term stay might be a nearby golf course or pickle ball courts or a bird sanctuary.

Picture yourself saying, "Yes, this looks like a place where we can be happy!"

Given our propensity for hanging out at this track facility nearly every morning, our stay in Mexico has presented certain lifestyle differences with our new friends. Never mind the differences of politics, religion, spending habits, eating habits, even reading habits. It's the mindset of daily physical workouts—as in aerobic and anaerobic repeats at a gym—the mindset we share with that reference group I described. So far, none of our Manzanillo friends in all these years have taken to a fascination for our community track in quite the same way. They do give the track a try now and then for their daily walks, but sooner or later they decide that their exercise can be better spent walking to the market. They even total up impressive steps each day in that way, and they are truly fit. Like good friends do when minor lifestyle choices arise, we all have found other activities to share.

As for our special group of running friends back home, true to the cause, they carry on as usual each Saturday without us. We cheer from a distance. And true to good friendships, they welcome our return in the spring.

Leaving like that as we did, in wild abandon for an extended stay, and especially in a foreign land, with no thought regarding social ties in the new life, can be downright risky. Homesickness can be the downfall of a misguided search for an exciting change. We know couples who sold all their belongings to start a new life in Mexico, only to learn that they were still chasing the dream. Marriages threatened, investments lost, health compromised—these are real. Beware.

But here's the really nice thing about a "reference group": It need not be singular. Sociologists tell us that more than one reference group, even multiple reference groups, are common for a majority of people. Wow, that was good news for us that first year when Mister Will and I did take off in hot pursuit of dreams, leaving our comfy home, our families, and our circle of friends to sample a new life away from everything Minnesotan. In our new setting, we did not know even one soul. That's where another reference group comes in handy.

Mister Will and I managed to escape the dire consequences of our impetuous decision because twists and turns channeled new friends into our Mexico life. That, of course, took time. I said we didn't know a soul, but that's not exactly accurate because our seller, remember Super Gal, was from our own home state no less. She stayed in the Posada picture through that next season because she simply didn't want to give up on Mexico or Posada. She rented the neighboring condo, smug in the fact that renting was the preferred way to go after all, with none of those nuisance and costly issues that owners saddle. Understanding now the full weight of ownership, I can imagine that she was ecstatic to experience life at Posada, but as a laid-back renter. She likely wanted to ease out of her Posada way of life, rather than depart abruptly, and decided that hanging on a bit longer as a renter surely would be fun. But that didn't work out so well when there, from her patio, she watched us ditching assorted furniture and furnishings from this condo that she so proudly had updated over her nine years of ownership. We were making Casa 4 ours, of course. She didn't return the next season. So we did have this one acquaintance, the disgruntled seller, Super Gal. Basically, you see, we were on our own.

We settled in that first year, minding our own business, as the other condo owners showed up for the season, one by one. Here's where a more thorough understanding of condo life would have served us well—even the most basic understanding of condo life. The concept of a shared community is what I'm getting at and especially in the case of a foreign culture. Our narrow-sighted focus had been simply to own a place on the ocean. Period.

Timing-wise, we didn't have a true picture of Posada when we made our purchase in that spring of 2005. Posada was basically empty, since the month was early April which means the North Americans had left for the season and the Mexicans had not yet arrived for their Easter (*Semana Santa*) holiday. Basically empty...and all ours. Immersed as we were in our own little world as proud owners, we didn't fully appreciate the quietness and the privacy of the particular time of year when we made the deal: "low season," as we know that term in vacation country. Of course, the place was empty! Did we not expect that others would eventually be there too? Did we not realize that at any given week, all of the units could be occupied, thus requiring a certain amount of agility in sharing the common spaces, as in the pool and gardens, the beach wall, the laundry? Did we not understand that neighbors, especially across from us and next door, might be aware of our every move from then on? Welcome to condo living.

So that first season we needed to adjust our thinking to a more expansive view of life at our Pacific home. Posada began to fill up. After all, this now was January, the height of the season for people like us. First showing up, I recall it was the couple from Iowa in Casa 1 directly across from us. They made a particular impression because they were loud and fun-loving, and notably very personable and welcoming to us, the new kids at the condo. Handshakes, hugs...we were instantly accepted. After we helped empty their pickup of all the stuff they too had hauled across the border—a tremendous amount of stuff by the way, including even a sofa bed, you know, the really heavy piece of furniture that no reasonable person without a lifting belt should lift—then they brought out the beer, and then more beer, and we became acquainted at their patio table. That, in fact, was the start of our drinking phase.

Either that day or a day or two later, a couple arrived all the way from British Columbia, a seven-day trip in their camper. We felt like slackers with only four days of bragging rights under our seatbelts. A truck driver by trade, this new neighbor considered such a trip common place. He and his wife settled in the one-bedroom unit next to Casa 1, their joining patios serving conveniently as party central. Then renters showed up, only known by first names, which upon reflection might have been by design... Merrill and Lolita, gypsies really, with connections to oil fields in Texas and a business in the Philippines, driving up in a messy old sedan. Raucous and sweet at the same time, jokes by the minute, Merrill and Lolita fit in like a missing cog to the celebratory drinking group. All relieved as hell to have landed at our Mexico destination after long trips, we folks at Posada del Sol toasted to our good fortune. *Salud!* This then would be the beginnings of our first Mexican "reference group": North Americans who winter in Mexico.

Through that first bumpy year or two, an unlikely acquaintance and one of these North Americans who winter in Mexico, helped us find our way in the strange new Mexican setting: George, a Texan, age ninety. George happened by at one of the drinking parties at Posada, a friend to some of the long-timers and a neighbor from just a few blocks away. George's story in Manzanillo began decades earlier, in the 1960s, when he left his job in Texas to roam Mexico on a motorcycle. Inquisitive and genuine with an easy smile, he was a free spirit. At that drinking party, amid the usual chit-chat, it was George who overheard our exasperated tale of computer hook-up problems. "Maybe I can help ya'll," he offered with a wide cowboy grin. "I'll stop by tomorrow."

And he did. Remember, this is a ninety-year-old who was solving our internet issues...along the lines of a "Senior Geek Squad." He couldn't wait to give us the low-down on computer capabilities and the latest uploads for music and then this: actual face-to-face chats with a new technology...back in those days, Skype.

Even beyond the computer, the three of us clicked and became fast buddies. Often, just a chat at George's place set us on a straight path again in dealing with one or another of the dramas beset us in condo living Mexican style. He showed us a lifestyle much wiser and looser than our buttoned-up approach. He expanded our bordered minds. And for me especially, he served as a fill-in for my dear dad whom I had recently lost. Ah, lovely George...we had him for another five years.

Church can matter too. The fact that few Lutherans reside in Mexico likely won't bother most, but for us from the good state of Minnesota with its northern European roots, well, Mister Will and I had to rethink our weekly attendance at worship: either attend a Catholic service, all in Spanish, and get out of it at least a churchy mood, or skip church entirely. We veered toward skipping entirely. So you good Protestants out there, take note, as well as you Catholics who would prefer English and wouldn't mind even an inter-denominational experience. Remember, think through what and who you are leaving.

For us with this church issue, a sign appeared from above—really, this was an actual posted notice above our table at our usual restaurant: "English speaking, nondenominational church, Sundays 5 p.m. at Pedro's on the Beach." That was our church answer. Not only did it solve the language issue, but potentially it could mean drinks and food at Pedro's. And it was just that: Under the shade of a *palapa* on Pedro's patio, we received a bit of scripture, prayer and song, then afterward we moved a few feet to the restaurant tables where we ordered up our margaritas and fajitas. A win-win for us; a win-win for Pedro. But dare I say, good Lutheran that I am, that a bit of mariachi music at a Catholic service—which I've heard does happen—might pull me there.

The church, oddly, was the connection for many more in our new reference group. I say "oddly," because here we were in our partying, finding-our-fun-selves mode and not particularly seeking anything social from a church service, of all things. In fact, our mega church back home had nearly drained us of all things "fellowship." We essentially were renegades in the church department. My thinking is that God, in all His wisdom, knew that we, with that bad taste still from the church back home, might need to be enticed with margaritas into another church setting. From that dozen or so people who gathered each Sunday evening at the beach, we branched out to more connections in the community. And beyond...my acquaintance with Judith, for instance, evolved into a Friday night supper group, most from that group having no connection whatsoever with the church. Our group has been bonding ever since, even to make visits when back at our homes in the States and Canada. Mister Will and I have evolved with that little congregation as it shifted to a more central focus away from Pedro's restaurant to an actual church setting but an hour farther up the coast. No problem, we say—a nice drive and more social connections.

And more social connections came our way through that fun-loving couple from Posada's Casa 1: They moved just a block up the bay to a larger condo, yet made sure that the much-cared-for Casa 1 would remain in the family by selling to a brother. They continue to draw friends from back home who fall in love with Manzanillo too, and so the friends-factor multiplies. Not unusual is a pool volleyball game where twenty-five people show up. And back to Casa 1, that brother with his wife continue the fun-loving Mexico tradition by packing in more family.

So then, our second reference group, we people who winter in Mexico, is diverse and colorful, but all with the common bond of Mexico. Whether sharing complaints or admiration for all things Mexican, we are drawn together. We could be tattooed with that distinction.

A reference group off-shoot perhaps is the Mexicans themselves. And here, obviously, speaking the same language is not necessarily of prime importance. For instance, at our *Cinco de Mayo* track each morning we greet the regulars and might share a word or two of our limited Spanish, even a hearty laugh at the mutual slips in translation, but basically, it's the unspoken that translates to friendship...the smile, the nod, the high sign or thumb's up or cheer for a good workout. Here again, like our reference group back home, it's a commune of sports-minded individuals. The list of track connections grows: Jorge, a storekeeper who sponsors a yearly race; Conrado, a realtor and his brother-in-law Josè, an air traffic controller; Fernando, a scuba teacher; Fernando's friend the veterinarian; Mariana and her husband Maurice who run a juice stand; their friend the exercise coach; Janet, who helps at the juice stand; Manuel, retired now after thirty years of track maintenance (bent and still smoking); and his two long-term groundskeepers, always with a smile who like to joke with us about a homeless cat gone missing, *"No gato."* No cat.

One of my favorite experiences of all time was participating in Manzanillo's triathlon, and this every day, community track was where I had the connection. On just a normal day of exercise, a local Mexican ran up from behind and asked, in fairly good English, if I would like to be part of a women's team with his wife of about my age. As he said with a cunning grin about the age comment, "Old...but in a good way." This was the first I'd seen of him, but apparently word travels in sprinting mode when teams such as this triathlon need a swimmer, a biker, or a runner like myself to fill the category...and especially so with respect to a women's team which, by the way, are few and far between in Mexico, macho as it is. So I had that top-of-the-mountain athletic experience out of the blue, and it came at just the right time...in the midst of a particularly bad round of homesickness. In my case, nothing works better for the doldrums than a race deadline with a dedicated training schedule. A cure. And all as a result of our humble track.

The "local Mexican" who ran up beside me that day was Conrado, who happens to be an avid runner himself, as well as a biker and swimmer and—very important to note—is a well-established, upscale Mexican realtor. His profession has become more relevant in recent years as we have asked the question, "What the hell are we doing owning property in Mexico anyhow?" More later about that. But you see the network that begins with just one conversation...first Conrado, then his wife, the family, the community. This is basic psychology, but with a twist of Spanish. This is where just trying the new language makes sense. Remember, the eighteen-inch challenge.

Even at Posada, with the almost daily challenges to harmonious condo living, our Mexican neighbors are part of our healthy social equation—another reference group. Bottom line for our Posada group: we all together are enjoying our Mexican getaway on the Pacific. Unfiltered from the condo setting which, Mister Will and I suspect, happens to accentuate a certain showmanship by the Mexicans for us foreigners to see; our Mexican owners have shown generous hospitality and admirable goodwill.

Especially striking is their giving of time. Example: When in passing I asked my Guadalajara neighbor for her enchilada recipe, she on that very day without hesitation and without notice shopped for the ingredients - including the distinctive *chiles guajillo entero*. Then she with great energy and enthusiasm showed up at my door with groceries in hand to demonstrate. We spent the afternoon in my *cocina* - and this was during her family's precious holiday time away at the coast. We north Americans who are so constricted with our personal schedules as to carry our calendars with us should take note: Loosen up.

Garnering up these new friendships in recent years - these new reference groups - Mister Will and I wonder now, how can we ever move on? This Mexico experience is who we have become. But we ask ourselves: Why not travel the world a trip at a time like so many retirees these days and avoid any long-term commitments? See places. The transitory nature of world travel certainly has an appeal for taking in sights, lots of them, as in the overly popular "bucket lists" theme—and we'd better hurry up before we die, that's the hook. And that's not to say friendships don't happen unless setting out for an extended time away. Even sporadic, short trips might include the exchange of name and address with a fellow traveler, but maybe not, depending on your personality type. My friend Betty exemplifies that outgoing personality who searches out friends, stays in touch, makes those binding ties; she and her husband in their many travels have long-term friends throughout the world. I look up to that.

In contrast, someone like myself prefers a settling-in that allows friendships to develop, even to coax out. Easily imagined is a one or two-week trip, here, there, without cause to form any bonding relationships. For me, that would be just another trip with photos of landscapes. Of special curiosity, I am noticing that people who vacation in Mexico for a short week or two do make a point to return but for a longer stay, and the next year, still a longer stay, all the while forming friendships. And soon they bring family and friends who begin their own journey in Mexico. Bonds form. Dare I suggest, do hold on to the idea of a long-term stay in Mexico. Hold on to those ties.

Chapter 13 – The Health Plan
Lesson: Know Your Happy-Life Prescriptions

Not to be confused with "health care" which we from the US for certain know to be a divisive and complicated political issue long to be debated, it appears, at the cost of, well, our health... Not to be confused with *that*, this is a look at Mexico as a place of simple healthy renewal. Mexico offers a welcome self-help prescription. Away from the noisy politicians, the alarming pharmaceutical ads, the rush of everyday living in our hurried lives back home, we can find a calm in Mexico as if by magic.

But, is Mexico the choice above all for retirement? A Google search will provide not one, but many lists of the worst and the best US states and places abroad for retirement...and no two lists are the same. They do share, however, these criteria of preference: low cost of living, temperate climate, access to health care.

So we study the possibilities. The question "What can I afford?" is closely followed by "Will I stay healthy to enjoy my retirement?" Then, for the financial planners to scrutinize, this twisted goal and ultimate puzzle: Make sure we don't outlive our money. Whoa, what if our calculation is off? If we worry about being left to the care and control of government assistance, then, I'm thinking, quite possibly we subconsciously let our health decline. Isn't a long, healthy life the bottom line?

Community seminars are made of these issues in today's ever-growing population of seniors. A financial planner entices us with "retirement tips": "How not to run out of money... How to spend less but keep your lifestyle... Plan on living longer than you expect." Another financial expert promotes a facility "that balances security and independence." We seniors like to know our options. Unlike most of our parents, who simply carried on in their own homes until one dark day when the nursing home was the only alternative, we have choices. So that's good.

In today's world of aging populations, "active-adult communities" is the living arrangement sought by well-funded seniors who choose to live and play among other people their age. Take for example, "The Villages," a Florida master-planned retirement community with upward of 82,000 fifty-five and older residents, where golf carts replace cars, life in the golden years is leisure, and the dress code is chic-casual. Self-promoted as "The Premier Active Adult Community," The Villages, at last count, has 89 swimming pools, 50 golf courses and over 2,400 organized clubs and activities. That's a lot of action.

Too much organized activity, you say? Too much la-tee-da? Well, in that case, there are more choices: the artist colonies, university-based communities, and a concept of "co-housing," where homes are clustered around a central courtyard and a common house. And let's not overlook an alternative that has been a choice for many decades: motor homes. Even house boats are in the mix. These creative options for the active adult are well worth noting—entertaining concepts in their own right.

But here's the winning card about Mexico: economics. The consumer price index tells us that the cost of living in Mexico is 40-50% less than in the United States and Canada. That, by my right-brain calculations, means we have 40-50% more time on this planet to spend our savings. That would signal a drastic turn in aging studies, do you agree? Well admittedly for this comparison, other issues about the where of retirement just might come into play, as in personal preferences for climate, housing, social ties, and so forth, but at least not the issue of financial concerns.

Those cost of living savings in Mexico come in the form of cheap and bountiful fresh fruits and vegetables, cheap transportation in buses and taxis, cheap medical care and drugs, cheap and skilled labor and craftsmen, and cheap dining, including even fine beach restaurants. In Mexico, any products that might seem slightly overpriced are, as expected, those imported items that we casually rely on at home: cosmetics, sun lotions, batteries, some appliances. But the basics of a very comfortable retirement life are easily affordable. Mexico is one of the destinations where living on Social Security is entirely doable.

A friend who actually tracks and compares his living expenses in Canada and Mexico claims that he and his wife return home every year after their five-month stay in Mexico with a sizable increase in their bank account to the tune of $5,000. That's US dollars, not pesos. Mister Will and I, though not micromanaging our costs to that degree, also notice an increase in our account. Can this be? We are paying our normal bills for our

Minnesota home and our expenses in Mexico—and essentially, we are coming out ahead by living in Mexico our three months. A growing number of Americans are retiring outside the US solely due to cost of living. Stretching dollars. We know a couple who sold their belongings in Minnesota and moved to Mexico because of excessive health insurance premiums. Another bought in Mexico because of excessive add-on costs at a senior development in California. And many more just because of overall lower costs, period.

Solving that part of the equation then, with financial worries out of the way, the focus is on healthy living in a temperate climate. Mexico has a good argument there as well: those fresh fruits and vegetables, so economical and plentiful at *el mercado*, become standard fare. Mexico doesn't seem to have "nutrition deserts," the term for US urban areas where the poor do not have easy access to fresh foods. Fresh produce abounds at the neighborhood open markets, as well as the big store chains, and even the stop-and-go establishments on side streets offer daily fresh ingredients for salsas. In a country like Mexico, where produce is more economical than processed foods, all consumers benefit nutritionally. So we eager foreigners from *el norte* take it all in like a super sale. Back home the prices are normally triple.

Climate is big. The southern temperatures of Mexico mixed with ocean air ease body tensions like a balm and naturally encourage outdoor activity. Our tight bodies relax, and we are ready to be active again. In the north, we hunker down in our houses for winter, which in Minnesota can mean five months of snow cover. Except for the hardy Scandinavian-types with skiing in their blood who see no reason to travel south anyway, snow is viewed as a limitation. We wait it out indoors, all for good reason: outdoors, the icy walkways threaten. Just one false move or quick turn on an icy surface could lead to weeks of recuperation, if not permanent disability. We seniors live with the fear that we might be just one broken hip away from a nursing home.

In Mexico, walking is a year-round activity, almost a must. Noteworthy too is that we foreigners do walk about freely in Mexico with little concern for safety, no more than if walking about in our home states. A walk might be to the *mercado* or to a restaurant or to the end of the bay just because. Maybe it's a hike to an overlook or a stroll on the beach to play with the waves. Now the handy devices that count steps engage a certain polite competition among friends for miles tallied in a day. Even rough estimates. "Oh, really....to the market and end of the bay, then back, then to the pharmacy and *tortilla* stand, oh and to the coffee shop...*that* far. " "Bring good walking sandals," is the advice Mister Will and I always give to our guests.

Socializing might not be your thing, but they say it's good for us—and Mexico offers lots of it. The Mexican open-air lifestyle on its very own encourages chit-chat, which at first seems excessive for those of us coming out of those hunkered-down houses of the north. Often in our Minnesota, we do not even intersect with our next door neighbors once our windows are closed in the fall and furnaces have started running for the long cold months ahead. From our house to our car to wherever our destination, then back, we do not need to speak with anyone really. That's a far cry, a shock actually, when we settle in at our coastal setting. As soon as the windows of our Casa 4 are flung open upon arrival, we seem fair game for anyone to stop by for a visit. Now promoted as a key component to a long life, social bonds come easily and frequently in the ocean climate, with fewer walls and fewer boundaries. Here recall my personal issues with the open-air lifestyle, so exposed it would seem, so in-your-face. But in the end, it's a true win for private me. I'm forging new friendships, enriched.

Add in Mexico's awe factor to the pluses of low cost and healthy lifestyle. The country of Mexico is astonishing. Mexico's geography, its climate, its people, its language, its customs... Mexico renews in us a sense of childlike wonder. Then toss in a magical mariachi ballad with all of the above as a backdrop, and there you have it: the awe-factor. That feeling of wonderment that is experienced regularly as a child often lessens as we age—this we are told by psychology majors. But research also tells us that the sense of wonderment, that awe we can easily spot in children, *can* be renewed and nurtured in us as seniors. If this feeling of wonder really does boost immunity as reported, well, that's like a double jackpot, wouldn't you agree? To add health benefits on top of the pure exhilarating joy of, say, an inspirational vista or tune, well, that's a lot of oxygen. The Mexico experience simply will not allow any other mindset. Our onbeat rhythms are shifted to syncopated, then back, the heart and soul of Mexico. We feel compelled to stop and take it all in, and we feel young again.

The effect of that tonic for youth was witnessed firsthand in our friend George, that ninety-year-old Texan with the penchant for learning. His curiosity and open-mindedness in the Mexican culture allowed a certain flexibility in his old body. Carrying on alone for twenty years after losing the love of his life, he wisely stayed connected to his Mexican community. Neighbors not only watched out for him; they were eager to take him into their families as one of their own. Both flourished.

That magnetic personality is what grabbed us too. Without failing, each time we visited, George taught us lessons on his Mexican way of life: from timesaving know-how in circumnavigating Mexico's immigration office, the tax system, the utilities, to practical approaches for our ongoing internet issues and simple everyday solutions, as in his "sand chair" maneuver when needing a place to sit on the beach for sunset. He absorbed the Mexican culture.

Remember that George was ninety years old nearing the end of his fifty-year lease on his home, when he signed the property over to a long-time friend with the understanding that George would live out his life in that home. The Mexican friend, because of her nationality, could own the property without a land lease.

In his last two years, George obtained his permanent Mexican status so that he could remain in Mexico year round. His choice was based on his failing health; he was well aware that returning to Texas would mean a permanent move to a nursing home. Instead, George took charge of his final years: He hired his own health aides for nominal pesos and with enormous benefits: a live-in woman with two young daughters. George benefited of course from on-site care, but he and the two girls benefited with their new cross-cultural, cross-generational ties. This scenario could certainly happen elsewhere, but in Mexico, it's commonplace. And in Mexico, labor is cheap.

We learned sadly that George did finally submit to a nursing home, but not far away in his beloved Mexico and only a few days before he died. The community of Lake Chapala near the city of Guadalajara is well known for its booming expat population and, with that, excellent medical facilities and nursing home care, all for a fraction of the cost of the States. That's where he lived out his final days.

US citizens and Canadians alike come to Mexico for less expensive health care. For one thing, most prescription medicines are available over-the-counter for half the price and with less fuss. And along with state-of-the-art medical facilities available nearby, Mexico continues the old-fashioned house calls. Especially for us foreigners not always sure about specific addresses in our area, the house call is welcome relief; it's a simple phone call for a doctor visit. Last year, when I struggled with a viral infection, Doctor Tom, as he is called, stopped by for a nominal fee to test for strep. Now with more medical products and technology available to Mexico's physicians, excellent ratings from patients are standard. We have firsthand reports from friends requiring urgent care who testify to excellent results for nominal fees. Often, the treating physician back home commends the treatment and gives the Mexican doctor a good grade. In treating our son-in-law's pneumonia one evening in the emergency room, the hospital charged only 200 *pesos*, about $20, and that covered a doctor's exam, tests, observation for three hours, medicines...and lunch. We were so thrilled with the outcome that in our hurry to leave, practically skipping out the door, we forgot to pay...as we left the building a nurse came running after us with the bill and a smile.

Dental work is especially popular with our Canadian friends, who specifically plan their appointments during their stay in Mexico. Canada does have privately owned dental plans but does not have government supported dental coverage. Our Canadian friend has even had extensive implants by his Mexican dentist to the tune of many, many *pesos*...still less than the cost back in Toronto. US travelers also take advantage of the low costs for dental cleaning and whitening. And for the occasional dental emergency, our secondhand reports are that Mexico knows its dentistry.

Given this supporting testimonial, still I admit my own reservations about Mexico's healthcare, but in the narrow category of sports medicine. When limping through a running injury, I chose to wait for my orthopedic specialist at home. That's me, hoping to magically work through the problem with no medical intervention whatsoever. Noticing over the years how Mexico has been behind, really, in the area of personal fitness workouts—for instance outdated calisthenics at the track, few hardcore runners, especially females—I have personally concluded that highly trained orthopedic specialists in athletic medicine might be difficult to find in Mexico, at least in our mid-size city of Manzanillo. But here again, Mexico's upswing in everything twenty-first century has likely leap-frogged my knowledge of medical resources in the area. In recent years, running races and triathlons seem to have gained tremendous momentum, reminding me of that surge in running events back home twenty years ago.

Meanwhile, I do know acquaintances who have had top-notch care, again inexpensive, for accidental injuries such as fractures and broken bones. Our neighbor who twisted her ankle crossing the median, quickly received care just blocks away. Another friend who suffered a broken shoulder in a bad fall on the sidewalk was shuttled to Guadalajara for specialty orthopedic care and ended up with even more than she expected: the surgeon noticed her torn rotator cuff and repaired that too. The unassuming Red Cross, *Cruce de Rojo,* is where our crusty George was treated when he took a fall from his kitchen stool. This all, to me, is reassuring.

Let me not forget to mention Josè, or "Holy Hands" as he likes to be known. Claiming to be trained in *kinesiocogo,* Josè, in his small messy *casa,* manipulates bodies even to walk again, or so we have heard from our gringo friends and acquaintances. Mister Will has given Josè a try or two in the case of hip or knee problems and has come away at least improved and with a keener sense of body harmony. Now isn't that what it's all about?

Health is a highly personal issue, and we travelers with a bent toward foreign places need to plan accordingly, then trust our instincts. We need to stay current with our health check-ups at home and respect any limitations, understand our prescriptions and their availability, and buy whatever insurance is out there that lessens our anxious moments about being far from our home medical providers. And, what if worse case you need to be transported back home? This type of protection in fact is what Mister Will and I recently purchased. SkyMed, it's called. We now can rest easy that, given a life-threatening medical situation, we will be transported to our hospital of choice in the US, and our family will not need to struggle with logistics and cost in addition to the worry about Mom or Dad. Peace of mind cannot be overrated.

Having addressed our particular health needs, our concerns, and any trepidation with unknowns in a foreign country...*then* we can carry on with our dreams. Mexico's enticement, of course, is in the prospect of a healthy, robust lifestyle complete with a net of medical services matching those at home, all at a modest price. Mexico has its own brand of active-adult community immersed in a kaleidoscope of Spanish culture keeping in step to a mariachi beat. Now that's a health plan.

Chapter 14 - *Viva Mexico*
Lesson: Trust Your Intuition

My discontent at Posada had a long simmer. You know how it is sometimes when you don't feel entirely comfortable in a new situation? In our case, at first the adjustment of this different lifestyle in a different country with a different language—and all quite suddenly—was daunting enough to assume that, of course, I might have some challenges. And I did. But I knew deep down that in due time, my unsettled nerves would eventually smooth out. Eventually. Think about it though; that's a tall order of change: lifestyle, country, language. Retirement in itself can present serious misgivings.

Change takes time. And in our case, there simply was no time to be rethinking our decision. On the go from sunrise to sunset, whether laboring to transform our Casa 4 or socializing with our new neighbors, we simply were carried along in this new wave. I did sense a moment or two of homesick melancholy early on, but that too would be drowned out by the incessant need for attention to something else. No time for quiet or contemplative assessment about this major overhaul in our lives.

Visitors took the edge off. Those first years when, conveniently, Sun Country flights were nonstop and dirt cheap, we hosted friends and family for one-week intervals spaced just enough apart for us to catch our breath. Then change the bedding, mop the floors, clean the bathrooms, and off to the airport to pick up the next batch. Think bed and breakfast, lunch and dinner, then toss in entertainment for a week. The taste of home they carried with them was so welcome and exhilarating that we couldn't help ourselves. As hosts in this exotic new land and feeling responsible and extremely proud to entertain, we poured it on with our self-made excursions not only in our city of Manzanillo, but up and down the coast. Remember, we have our car. Tours of the impressive Manzanillo port, visits to turtle and iguana sanctuaries, trips to special beaches for snorkeling and boogie-boarding, deep-sea fishing, boat rides in the mangroves, shopping at local markets, sightseeing at ruins and historical centers—we did it all, topped off with a touristy Mexican fiesta at one of the fancy hotels. Our guests didn't know enough to assume anything other than this version of hosting in Mexico. Any extra minutes for the obvious attractions, as in leisure by the pool or walks on the beach, were squeezed in before heading out again in the car. And the next guests had the same treatment. Repeat the vacation-hosting agenda.

By the end of any given week with guests, all of us housed in Casa 4 were done in. Our weary guests boarded their flights home, sunburned and exhausted; Mister Will and I hurried back from the airport to our casa for a long nap. Here's where Super Gal, our off-the-wall seller back in 2004, did have one piece of good advice about hosting which now makes perfect sense: Point all guests to the beach, the pool, the hammock, the refrigerator, and say, "Go for it!" Then relax without a worry about entertaining. Let guests do their own thing and experience for themselves the luxury of no schedules. Bottom line: travelers from the north are content just to thaw out for a week. Or, as our motto now is: "Chill in the heat."

But then again, to me, a good host goes a tad bit further. After all, in a foreign place especially, a little guidance is helpful. Language comes to mind. Even my own limited Spanish goes a long way when helping our guests with their souvenir purchases or menu choices. Some savvy guests even ask to try the local bus system for the fun of it and to learn their way around...on their own. And frankly, for a full immersion into Mexico, there's nothing quite like a local bus ride. So, that's the, other side of hosting… more freewheeling if our guests are up to it. Basically, now Mister Will and I operate on a guest-by-guest basis. Many years into this, we might take that advice from our seller, but only if our guests are repeats, plus come equipped with a word or two of Spanish. Even then, we find ourselves tagging along, not to miss anything.

So our guests kept us on the move. Then, several years ago, a quirk of fate stepped in to help us rethink our time at Posada del Sol: Sun Country Airlines *stopped* its flights to Manzanillo. That drastic change meant expensive, hobbled-together flights to reach our destination. Result: no guests. *Nada.* Obviously, travelers look for other vacation options when a one-week vacation is winnowed down by overnights to and from and the cost is nearly doubled. Even our family members decided that a Manzanillo trip was out of the realm. What? Not even our family will visit?

With this dramatic drop in our hosting duties, Mister Will and I had this extra time on our hands: time to get a feel for our Casa 4, our Posada del Sol, our Manzanillo, our Mexico. What were we to do with our days without guests in mind? Was there more to our life on a Mexican coast than tourist attractions? And the really important question: How could we justify spending three entire months away from home and family?

First and logically, our small Casa 4 became much bigger in our eyes, with just the two of us rattling around in our 800 square feet. Without our spare bedroom in regular use, we began to see the space for more than storing beer and extra boxes. An office of sorts took shape. And with that office space, our separate work areas expanded. Updates with cabinets and furniture were on our to-do list. We settled in more or less to yet a different lifestyle, where we were just fine on our own in our beachfront world. Now we experienced a luxury, really, for us so conditioned to hard work and over-active schedules.

This new abundance of time opened our world to spend time with our local friends. Now that we weren't shuttling off with guests on a regular daily basis, spur-of-the-moment visits with our Manzanillo friends became routine. Instead of the typical tourist attractions on our agenda over the years with our visitors, we ventured into unplanned events on the local scene, scouting out back streets to find neighborhood activities. We began to think of ourselves as locals. This freed-up lifestyle in our Casa 4 would be just fine, we agreed, and even therapeutic. "Look what we have been missing!" was our surprise reaction. "We most definitely can do this kick-back mode." This was the "us in Mexico" we pictured back on our first trips—remember the laid-back couple we longed to be? As for the tourist attractions of crowded beaches, the boogie-boarding, the snorkeling, the dive boats, the sunset cruises...those activities would be on hold until required again when visitors returned

Now then, to explain further, this cut-back in visitors was only specific for us who relied on a specific charter airline flying out of Minneapolis direct to Manzanillo. This change in flights by our carrier Sun Country, which was so dramatic for us from Minnesota, did not necessarily affect travelers from other areas of the US and Canada. That meant that our neighbors merrily continued to host their family and friends. Mister Will and I watched from our patio. As the visitor newbies wheeled their luggage in and out, pale-skinned and tightly wound at arrival, tanned and loose at departure, we watched. Whether Mister Will and I said it or not, we each wished for one or two of our own pale-skinned, tightly wound visitors.

But hosting vicariously works wonders. In our open-air little Posada community, everyone's presence is felt...and heard. The extra level of visitor chatter and laughter and splashes in the pool throughout their stay add a playfulness to our common areas. The oos and ahs from the US and Canadian visitors as they cast their view on the mighty Pacific clearly refocus us on the specialness of our winter spot. This is where we live three months a year. "Did we win the lottery?" We grin big. Certainly and without a doubt, despite our envy for visitors of our own, we sense a bit of relief during these periods when our North American neighbors are hosting...relief that we are not the ones responsible to entertain nonstop during our precious winter time away. We do quietly hope for a stray guest now and then.

Guests, it turns out, also serve a helpful purpose as a distraction or buffer to condominium ruckuses. Simply avoiding the hot issue of the day works extremely well under the cover of "We are too busy—we have guests." Not to say we intentionally neglect our responsibilities as owners, but when sides play against each other with trifling, underhanded comments, well, we have tried to steer clear, even if it means ducking behind our guests.

Over the years all of these distractions were fine and dandy for avoiding the real question on my own personal life-satisfaction quiz: Do I really like it here in Mexico? As mentioned, my discontent had been brewing and now was up to a slow simmer. Why was this Mexican dream life so difficult? How would I pinpoint the problem? What exactly put me on this wildly swinging emotional pendulum with enough downswings to awaken me at night in a cold sweat? Was it just the close quarters of open-air condo living with *cero* privacy? Was it our dysfunctional cross-cultural condo organization? What about our dirty air from the thermoelectric plant—was that it? Or, how about our embarrassingly antiquated plumbing?

And let's not forget the surge in remodeling by our Mexican owners. Honestly, Mister Will and I did not see this coming, and for me stewing about life satisfaction at Posada, the changes were confusing. Modern, and sleek, the Mexican *casas* took on a look of "House Beautiful," well, relative to old-style Posada. We now sensed being the poor house on the block. The latest in kitchen and bath appliances, sleek windows and doors...this was the trend. "Hmm, that's a switch," we privately thought. Much of Posada was under change. And where did we fit in?

I give Mister Will credit for his level head when these matters surface of unsettling condo relations and my emotional setbacks. If the conflict is with the *Mexicanos*, he plays his architect card with a professional business approach directly to the men. Maybe the issue still stands, as with the push and shove arguments on building additions to individual condos, but the *Mexicanos* respect another man speaking up and standing his ground; Mexico is a macho country, that's common knowledge.

If, from another stance, the conflict is with us North Americans, Mister Will plays his laid-back card with a friendly gesture, as in sharing a beer over talk about fishing. Again with the men, but well, why not in the name of cultural norms? I just look on in wonder. And if dealing with my super sensitive nature, his rational, common-sense, logical take on any of the issues calms me like the rhythm of lapping waves. He'll give me a hug and say, "Oh, don't worry about it for a second; we're just going to be ourselves just like always." So, Mister Will is the rock in all this drama. But this ever-growing tension, this build-up to drastic action, needed to be resolved, and the two of us needed to be of one mind. Mexico, *si*? Mexico, *no*?

As it happens sometimes, events out of our control act as messengers. When one of our Posada units suddenly popped up that second story, my monitor of grievances shot up also to a new anxious level. That's how abrupt it seemed...popped up like a pop-up trailer. When we left for Minnesota that spring, nothing was unusual about The *Don*'s Casa 8...same basic one-level modest casa like the original units at Posada del Sol. But when we returned in December, Casa 8 had been transformed into a two-level *casa grande*. This was not the do-it-yourself-type house update; this was the design of a well-funded architect and the work of a well-funded contractor: modern and beach stylish, complete with a thatched roof. First class.

Most important to note is the fact that such a two-story renovation by all Posada standards, no matter how classy, was against the rules. The basic look of Posada, the lovely grounds, the one-story roof line, was to be appreciated for its simple, old character charm. At least, that's what we from *el norte* understood, and for certain we from *el norte* couldn't even imagine a second story at our 1969 Posada. At no time, at least on our

English radar, was The *Don*'s intention made known to significantly reconstruct his Casa 8.

The *Don*, remember, was the wealthy businessman—as in numerous oil and gas ventures—one of the first Mexicanos who purchased at Posada. His unit directly on the ocean front was common like the rest, and we saw him only occasionally when he arrived by motorcycle for a day or two at his beach property, sometimes accompanied by young women of questionable reputation, or so we guessed. That's how it was with The *Don*... no frills, no interaction with us...he was just a wealthy, eccentric *Mexicano* who, incidentally and surprisingly, was always current paying his condo fees. So we never worried about him.

This is where paying fees on time doesn't necessarily forgive a blatant condo infraction, no matter who. We other owners gasped and sputtered over this flagrant violation of two levels not only to the rules but to us as owners and neighbors. "How could he do this without consulting us? *Amigos*?" we stewed. All along we had considered him a pretty decent guy.

We as an association of sorts considered a penalty, a payback, at least a penitent owner. But in the end, the now two-story luxury condo remained free and clear, towering above the rest in all its splendor. At our annual meeting, we owners intently listened to our gentlemanly *Mexicano* president at the time (the contractor from The Family) as he urged that all of us remain neighborly as Posada del Sol was intended, in spite of one owner's bad judgment. Neighborliness above all else, was his message. To that, The *Don*, in a show of unprecedented arrogance and haughtiness, informed the group that he didn't come to Posada for neighborliness—he came to Posada for the ocean front.

So that was that. We shuffled back to our respective units, and no more was said. Except...now Posada had a two-story structure that not only broke the aesthetic continuity of our

Posada roofline, but blocked some of the breezes and cast shade on the pool. When the topic does come up as it does regularly in tune with the sea breezes and cast of the sun, we owners fuss about the detestable two-story and rehash the details, but ultimately slink back into our chairs and concede, "Well, to be honest, The *Don*'s place does look very nice...and it probably raises our own property values here at Posada."

But the notion of property values wasn't foremost on my mind when the *concreto* dust settled and my anxiety level was at that new high. The effect of sea breezes was. There we were in our little Casa 4 tucked back and away from the seawall by some twenty yards, a good location to protect from a pounding surf, yet open enough to allow the circulation of breezes. As our realtor at one point praised, "You are on the ocean, but you're not." Now with this new double-high structure looming like a beach fortification, our air circulation at Casa 4 took on a distinct lull. I was hot. All the time. Sure, the other nagging concerns of my discontent likely contributed to my general physical discomfort, but adding the heat factor made for an unstable condition. And to agitate further, The *Don* now brought his large guard dogs, mostly a wolf breed we surmised, when he visited Posada. Again, another Posada no-no: Dogs are not welcome, especially menacing breeds on guard at our lovely seawall. Naturally, we other owners at Posada opted out of our sunsets at the seawall when faced with skirting the threatening dogs to get to our wall. The general tone at Posada turned fretful.

Now here is where life and all its drama sometimes gives us pause to reflect. Never, ever, intentionally or not, to wish ill of any sort—much less death—on anyone, anywhere, any time, we gringos received shocking news that next year and suddenly felt a dark sense of payback: The *Don* in fact died. Really, truly, we didn't know the extent of his illness, so absorbed we were in the reality of this two-story debacle forever with us at Posada. The *Don*'s intent for his *casa* redo, perhaps well-thought-out, likely was to provide a lovely ocean getaway for his large family. Who will ever know? The second-story coup now is just another piece of Posada's bizarre history.

And the second-story coup was one of those events out of our control. Looking back, I can see now that the second-story fiasco set in motion, like a Mexican hat dance, our quest to settle the dilemma once and for all. Mister Will and I asked ourselves: How could our fortuitous purchase in 2004 at an opportune moment in our lives transform into a wrong step—including a certain amount of misery—on life's road to retirement? Were we too impulsive in search of the good life? Too naive? And why all the struggles? This give and take, this courtship with Mexico...was it really love?

In January 2014, almost ten years from the date of purchase and just a year after the two-story debacle, Mister Will and I sat down for a hard talk with our track friend, the Mexican realtor I spoke about. We wanted to know with absolute certainty the worth of our Casa 4. We wanted to know about available properties in the area. We wanted to know how to proceed. And we hoped that this realtor friend, like the great authority from above, would have the right answer specifically for us.

Weeks before, as Mister Will and I sat at the sea wall looking out at the vast Pacific while contemplating our future in Mexico, we pictured ourselves happy simply in changing our view...literally. Let me explain: Initially, I had considered that we continue in Manzanillo but as renters, like many of our friends. Why subject ourselves to the worries of homeowners? The fees, the maintenance, the organizational duties, the worries, the dreaded annual meeting in two languages—why mess up a relaxing retirement? "Cripes, let's just rent and take it easy,"

I pleaded. But Mister Will would have nothing of it. Owning in Mexico has always been his thing.

We knew for certain that Mexico was our intended place, that was a given, having first tossed around the numerous options of warm-weather retirement spots in the US "Too bland, too so-so, too not-us," we agreed like two misfits in a retirement survey. And we knew for almost certain that the city of Manzanillo was the place for us. We liked the fact that Manzanillo still really hadn't caught on in the tourist world. We liked the rough edges. So, the question then was: Where in Manzanillo might we own that could bring us true happiness? This is where that change of view grabbed our attention.

The newer condos in recent decades have been oriented with views to the ocean, whereas our 1960s Posada del Sol was oriented around the swimming pool, thus, our Casa 4 faces not to the ocean but to the units across the pool. Could it be, we reasoned, that a forty-five-degree shift might make all the difference? Our friends renting or owning places with the ocean view seemed thoroughly content to sit for hours staring at the waves, the boats, the birds, the whales, the horizon. Seems not only reasonable but obligatory. Compared to that, our slot to the Pacific from our patio, some twenty yards away and at an angle, seemed, well, distant. A convincing argument can be made for that distant ocean view (see Chapter 9: Owning, Part 3) being safer, quieter, cleaner, and absolutely contributing to much less rust, but at this decision point, Mister Will and I could only think of the ocean as an obvious answer to our problem.

A second benefit to this orientation shift, albeit a touchy subject, would be privacy: no more neighbors peering from across the pool, or for that matter, no more us peering at them. Just the ocean and us, that's how we pictured our new selves straight on with the mighty Pacific. This benefit, however, would remain under cover, very hush-hush, as we searched for our new spot because, after all, how could we explain our need for privacy to our co-owners at Posada without implying nosiness? We *do* have great affection for our neighbors.

So, the process began. When we learned that our modest Casa 4—with minimal and very basic updates over those ten years, I must add—might even bring a profit, Mister Will and I quickly conjured up a new scenario: With only a little extra cash thrown in, relatively speaking, we could buy a slightly newer unit, with an ocean view, and without the baggage of our old Posada del Sol. And privacy besides.

When we shared this bit of condo intrigue with our friends, also owners themselves just down the bay, we were in for a big surprise: They were in the selling mode too, although unannounced, and oh, by the way, would we be interested in buying their unit? Over the years, the four of us had shared our tales of woe about condo ownership in Mexico, as in Mexican owners who are delinquent in payments and/or are disruptive, maintenance personnel who are unreliable and/or unhandy, structure problems which are costly and/or are not presently worth the effort, the list drags on like a line of traffic at the border. This offer out of the blue was even with assurance that they would be content to wait however long need be for ours to sell. Really? Mister Will and I hurriedly did the math again. Eking out a slight profit from our Casa 4 and throwing in an extra few thousand, we could make the numbers—and our new vista in Manzanillo—work. Just that easy, we too could have an ocean view in a newer unit.

Mister Will and I had a new spring in our step. No longer were we worried where we might land; we only needed *to sell*. Our Casa 4 officially was listed. There on the Coldwell Banker website we studied the flattering description, half sorry to be letting go of our Casa 4 now in this new bright light, yet relieved to have our new plan in motion. Finally, we were on the move. But the motion was slow, as is reasonably assumed in Mexico. We waited long weeks to hear of any action. It wasn't until that summer, of course then back in Minnesota, when we had a call from our realtor friend that, in fact, he had a potential buyer. Then soon after, another, and another. Ironically, our very own condominium regulations, or our condo neighbors' standards at least, posed a stumbling block: the damnable no-second-story rule. These potential buyers saw jazzed-up potential in adding a second-story bedroom or even just an open terrace to our humble Casa 4. Just a slight structural adjustment with a winding staircase to the rooftop, no big issue—that was the idea. Okay, we get it: the view to the Pacific would be tremendous. But, "No," we dutifully replied. "Our condo rules don't allow a second story."

Still, we waited for the right buyer: "Maybe a couple just like us," we dreamed, content in waiting out the process as we carried on usual fashion in our *"coqueto"* Casa 4, which now took on for us a subtle attraction and charm. Flirtatious. With an update in the wings if we could swing the deal for our friends' condo, we were comfortable just as we were and secretly tickled by the thought of a second-story *terraza* on our little Casa 4.

That second season of the listing produced more lookers but, subconsciously no doubt, now that I rethink our motives and behavior, Mister Will and I orchestrated subversive tactics to rule them out. For instance, when prospects were skeptically eyeing our tired and worn windows, our old refrigerator, our rust-tarnished kitchen sink, and whatever else presented as seriously dated, we heartily agreed. "You are so right—this place could use some updates." We nodded. If perhaps they were already renting at a condo and just considering the market to own, we talked up the various fees associated with owning, with the not-so-subliminal message: Why do foreigners own when they can rent without all the hassle, for heaven's sake? What we said was something like, "Yes, our fees have remained quite high but our association has had to catch up with basic maintenance. That happens."

And at about that same time, our good Canadian neighbor who loves Mexico with all her heart, and who by the way is frightening sometimes in her mood swings (the same one who hacked down an ill-placed palm tree on the beach), now in a rage about the plight of Posada del Sol should our Casa 4 sell to the wrong buyer, climbed a ladder in plain sight at the Posada gate and tore down our Coldwell Banker for-sale sign! Mister Will and I, shocked and angered, but then touched with a pang of tenderheartedness for that neighbor, could only shake our heads and wonder, "Could this mean she really likes us after all and wants us to stay?"

Another undercurrent was tossing us about: Our commitment to our friends with their condo on hold. Sure, their unit was lovely and meticulously maintained with a fantastic ocean view and with the perfect location near our famously dear track. Their unit would be a giant step up from our dated Posada del Sol Casa 4. But could we remain friends? Wouldn't they always be hypercritical of our designing ideas? Mister Will and I already were envisioning our own decorating preferences, complete with bright painting schemes, which might come across as drastic and dismissive to our friends' more subdued taste. As the generality goes, many Canadians are under-spoken. So, we worried.

And one more consideration about this change: This giant step *up* for us in buying our friends' newer, fancier condo would also mean in fact thirty-six actual steps just to get in the door— a third-floor condo rather than our ground-level condo. Now that's a hike, especially carrying groceries, luggage, what not. Mister Will and I began to picture various older friends from home opting *not* to visit us solely because of the steps; plus let's face it, we weren't getting any younger. In fact, that year I, who for the most part have been immune from running injuries my whole life, turned up with a slight knee issue (call it intervention) which brought home the reality of climbing excessive stairs. Active me, of all people, with a knee problem. So, the question lingered: Why would a couple in their seventies choose to buy a condo on the third floor with no elevator? We pondered.

Then, a sign. That April, which is late in the season for us, our daughter and her family visited. They had visited various other years, but this visit would be a two-week stay rather than just one week, and they would rent a place on their own and get the feel of regulars, which intrigued them. The two grandkids now were teenagers, so our small second bedroom no longer could accommodate the family. As small children, the two grandkids fit nicely on an inflatable mattress tucked between the two single beds. But no more. So, the family rented, coincidentally, and ironically, and I've got to believe, providentially, at the condos where Mister Will and I had our secret deal in waiting. We were very proud to have our family in this nicer, newer (by several decades) space, savoring the knowledge that in just a matter of time we in fact would be owning one of those condos. The ocean view would soon be ours.

As I said, April was late in the season for us, so by then we were ready to shut down and get in our car for Minnesota. And with the past months overshadowed by the listing and showings and uncertainty of our future in Manzanillo with no foreseeable sale in the works, we considered taking Casa 4 off the market for the summer months. After all, who buys Mexican beach property in the summer? We were in a state of limbo.

And then, in the midst of all this frustration and worry, the hassle, the doubt, the hair-pulling concerns, came this crystal-clear sign about our future: A simple, unbiased comment about comfort. During that week when our family rented down the bay in the newer complex, our granddaughter Bella told her mother offhandedly, as only a teenager can do, "I like Grandpa and Grandma's place better."

My voice shot up an octave. "Really? She said that?" We let the words sink in….and then quizzed Bella's mother again. "Really? Say it again, but more s-l-o-w-l-y."

Normally, a comment like hers might go unnoticed in another setting, but with Mister Will and myself both on high alert for any hint whatsoever as to where we should be in Mexico, or for that matter in the universe, my goodness, well, the comment hit like Mexican fireworks. It was as if after a grand crescendo, a brilliant light had suddenly appeared above all of Posada del Sol and the mariachi trumpets were sounding! Mister Will and I teared up. We hugged. We hugged again.

Wow, we didn't see that coming. Bella's words suddenly brought to light a new vision. We wondered, "Could this mean that our little Casa 4, so old and needing repair, is actually where we ought to be?" All of our efforts thus far with our casa on the market had been directed to finding somewhere *else*…still in Manzanillo, but newer, classier, better…somewhere *else*. Any thoughts about staying at Casa 4 had petered out with this latest condo upheaval. But could it be that all we needed was a loving affirmation about our little Casa 4?

Now, with this bell-ringing comment from a 15-year-old, we were shocked into considering yet another possibility, a possibility there all along. Our thoughts, as if on steroids, pivoted to "What if?" What if we updated our forty-year-old windows? What if our front wall were modified just slightly to catch more of the ocean air? What if we added more plantings along our patio to personalize and screen our space? What if that abominable angel were removed from our wall? What if, after ten years with minimal updates and even ghosts of owners past, we finally made Casa 4 our own? As seen through this new lens, Casa 4 took on an extraordinary value: our wellbeing.

The exercise in listing our property did pay off. By now we were fully in tune with the market attractions of our economical Casa 4 with the growing trend for walk-outs, the uniqueness of a large patio, the draw of a vibrant location, the lovely grounds. Check, check, check, check. We had become well aware of these pluses in this exercise of selling. But the affirmation of family at this crucial time was priceless. All the while that Mister Will and I had been anguishing over bigger and better, newer and thoroughly modern, it was our unassuming little casa in all its funkiness that endeared. We were smitten again.

That April 2015, the Coldwell Banker sign came down again, for good. Mister Will and I packed the Toyota to head north, but this time clear-eyed with a joyful resolution in mind and an eagerness to return. Casa 4 would be waiting there for us. Whatever adventure might await us, we would welcome it as if setting out on our first trip to Mexico.

The mariachi dancers strike their heels with gusto. *Ole!*

Epilogue

The "what-ifs" did happen. The update of Casa 4 really did make a difference. Though mostly a facelift to the front side of our casa, the effect was a spacious feeling throughout. Ingenious architect Mister Will designed a winged kitchen wall which in effect gained us a window to the ocean without impinging on common condo property. How's that, you say? Well, our addition stayed within our patio space, the footprint allowed by the condo association.

Then with the new sliding windows along the front, the glass door, new shower doors, and new, thoroughly modern ceiling fans, four of them, the place took on a much younger spirit. Or was that us?

The angel over our bed did come down. Praise the Lord! Secured as it was with rebar, the concrete form had withstood even the frequent earthquakes in this region. We imagined that removal certainly would involve a hacksaw, hammers and chisels, leaving the worldly seraph in a huge pile of pieces on the floor. Dust to dust. We didn't stay that year to watch our contractor do the deed but instead headed home while he tended to various other repairs as well. But she came off the wall clean, we were told. And quite possibly she lives on, so the report goes. *La Angel,* as we called her, was deposited next to the dumpster in the alley, only to mysteriously disappear when next checked upon. As if into thin air, it would seem. The question lingers: Now, where is she casting her spell?

This contractor friend, by the way, an expat from Canada, in effect rescued us with his wherewithal and fluent Spanish in working seamlessly with the Mexican trades to get done whatever it is we needed...the wall, the windows, the angel, etc. We keep his number handy by our phone.

So, we carry on at our Posada del Sol in Manzanillo, Mexico, content with our original investment in Casa 4...our flirtatious Casa 4. An ongoing list of improvements is paper clipped to the calendar, but no hurry, we say. Consideration must be made for parsing out days or even weeks to accomplish the projects, when our time in Mexico is limited each year. We rationalize: Who, with any sense of play and joy and with a set number of days in Mexico, undertakes yet another casa project which can only translate to less time for play and joy? In this way of thinking, we have continued the improvements, but with an eye for high impact/low hassle.

Meanwhile, challenges persist: In a recent year, our Posada manager absconded with condo funds, leaving the account basically empty. That dire situation has slowly improved, thanks to a newly appointed top-notch manager and a professional accounting firm, but still, we agonize over collecting fees. Next, our Casa 4 roof—the 60-year-old concrete/rebar roof with signs of rust and deterioration—had to be replaced. Yes, the entire roof jackhammered off and a new roof poured. Now, we worry about the neighbor's adjoining roof. Next, Dear Roque, after nearly twenty years of faithful service to Posada, says he will be retiring soon. Who can ever fill his shoes? We worry. And most recently, a hurricane took out part of our seawall, and certain Posada owners refuse to pay their share for the repair. Please tell me, how can we owners agree on anything if not the seawall there to protect us? With challenges like these, Mister Will and I reflect on a Spanish word that is often cheered at running races: "*Animo!*" Translation: Courage to carry on.

An airline promotion probably says it best when it comes to selling others on the idea of Mexico: "Live Mexico to Believe

It!" That goes for the good and not-so-good, I suppose, but here again, this is my story and I am confident that I've given enough attention to those not-so-good issues. What I'm getting at are those glimpses of Mexico that speak to me. No amount of testimonials, recommendations, advice, coaching, warning, or personal-travel-guide narrative can capture a life in Mexico. What's needed are those firsthand sensory glimpses: *To see* the vibrant hues of bougainvillea, hibiscus, and desert rose picked up in the hues of Mexican native dress, *to smell* the warm tortillas fresh from neighborhood *tortillarias, to taste* the distinctive cilantro in fresh salsa *Mexicano* served with *tostadas* and freshly baked *bolillos, to touch* the fine wool *sarapes* and blankets at market...and *to hear* the distinctive sounds of *mariachi* music, the heart and soul of Mexico.

Ah, the *mariachi*. Dating back to at least the 18th century, the music has evolved over time in the countryside of various regions of western Mexico. In the 20th century, the music transformed from rural to urban and then came to represent Mexico. The origin of the word mariachi, some say, is from the name of the wood used for the dance platform. Others say it's the name of a tree, or an image. I particularly like the long-held theory, a more romantic one, that the name was associated with the French word for marriage. That theory dates back to the French intervention in Mexico in the 1860s and the fact that the mariachi has always been popular at weddings. That theory, however, was disproven in 1981 when a document revealed that the word existed long before the French invasion: In 1848, Father Cosme Santa Ana wrote to the archbishop about the mariachis. Still, I hold that the French did have their influence.

With the contrasting sounds and shifting rhythms of trumpets, violins, guitar, *vihuela, guitarron,* and gusto male vocals, the indigenous *mariachi* sound excites and enchants. Often implemented to celebrate great moments in the lives of ordinary Mexican people, the music over the centuries has been both utilitarian and entertainment, even incorporated into the Roman Catholic mass. How better to celebrate Lord of Ascension Sunday than with uplifting sounds of mariachi joining uplifting prayers of the people. Is it any wonder that the mariachi will bring a smile or a tear or a tapping of the toe? Is it any wonder that music is less misinterpreted than words?

For me, those firsthand sensory glimpses I mention bring Mexico into focus, as if framing the gentle giant into a keepsake pose. Despite all of the fears, the worries and frustration, the setbacks, the challenges and misgivings, and despite our own US warnings and patrol of the border, these everyday glimpses into our *Mexicano* neighbors encapsulate the magnetic pull of Mexico.

And then the sixth sense: To feel in my gut—*to just know*—that Mexico is right for us, Mister Will and me. Is it no surprise then, that the word "mariachi" for me will always summon up romance? And that's why we remain proud owners of our Casa 4 at Posada del Sol in Manzanillo, Mexico. The colorful and romantic stories will continue, and Mister Will and I will take on the adventure hand in hand.

Acknowledgments

Above all, thank you, Wilt, for believing in this project. Your encouragement, patience, and loving advice kept me going. You inspired me in some instances to see a matter in a whole new light: rationally! You never once complained about reading through the manuscript just one more time..."please, this is the last draft, really...." I am so blessed that we are life partners and travel partners. This remarkable Mexico adventure is ours forever, with *amor.*

Thank you, Sally and Tacho, for your important cross-cultural work with mission teams through the years. Your thoughtful planning to ensure well-rounded and meaningful trips for volunteers has provided an invaluable groundwork for appreciating the true richness of Mexico.

Thank you, Shelby, for the keen vision you and Jim promoted all those years ago for Volunteers On Leave To Serve. And thank you for your word "refirement."

Thank you, those who read *Mariachi* for feedback: Molly, Betty, Harold, Jamelle, Sally, Tacho. Along the way, you also edited and pointed me to areas for further thought on cultural awareness. I am grateful.

Thank you, Mike, for your gentle prompts to stay creative, always.

Thank you, Saturday Morning Running Group, for your steadfast friendship and energy all these decades as we have circled the lakes and for your ongoing support whenever I have rattled on about my writing projects.

Thank you, kids and grandkids, for helping me learn the many roads of social media.

Thank you, my Posada *amigos*, for your trust. We really are family.

Thank you, Ann and your editing team at Kirk House Publishers, for your professional care and energy in getting my story out. Praise to small presses!

And thank you by way of heart-felt remembrances to those we lost over the years who had special connections with Manzanillo, forming the memories I hold dear. Each played a lasting part in my story.

About the Author

For over 30 years, Faye has frequently traveled in Mexico, and for the last 18 years she has wintered there. Her love of Mexico began when she and her husband worked with the Mazahuan people on the high plateau out of Mexico City. That love carried them along years later to the adventure of owning property on the Pacific coast, all the while learning on the go.

Faye has a Bachelor of Science degree from the University of Minnesota. Her volunteer interests have included Families Moving Forward, Good Samaritan Nursing Homes, and the Twin Cities Marathon.

She is the author of *Gumption, Lessons on Old Age, Loneliness, and a Hotdish* (2010), a true tale about the resilient spirit of old men in her small hometown in Minnesota. She has made numerous presentations on the subject of "positive aging." She wrote a piece under that title for *Minnesota Women's Press* (2011).

Faye also wrote *Finding Foxholes, a World War II Infantry Route, Then...and 48 Years Later* (2014) combining her travelogue with coinciding audio-taped stories by her father, a Bronze Star, World War II infantry soldier. In 2016, she was honored as the speaker at the Memorial Service in Renville, MN. In 2017, *Finding Foxholes* was selected for the One Book One County reading program by the Minnesota Arts and Cultural Heritage Library Legacy Fund.

In 2006, Faye's "South of the Border" was featured in *Running Times*.

Faye and her husband live nine months a year in Minneapolis, MN and three months in Manzanillo, MX. They have four children and seven grandchildren.

CPSIA information can be obtained
at www.ICGtesting.com
Printed in the USA
BVHW030850200822
645080BV00008B/388